Alfred Essa and Shirin Mojarad
Practical AI for Business Leaders, Product Managers, and Entrepreneurs

Alfred Essa and Shirin Mojarad

Practical AI for Business Leaders, Product Managers, and Entrepreneurs

—

DE GRUYTER

ISBN 978-1-5015-1464-7
e-ISBN (PDF) 978-1-5015-0573-7
e-ISBN (EPUB) 978-1-5015-0584-3

Library of Congress Control Number: 2021949660

Bibliographic information published by the Deutsche Nationalbibliothek
The Deutsche Nationalbibliothek lists this publication in the Deutsche Nationalbibliografie;
detailed bibliographic data are available on the Internet at http://dnb.dnb.de.

© 2022 Walter de Gruyter Inc., Boston/Berlin
Cover image: peepo / E+ / gettyimages.de
Typesetting: VTeX UAB, Lithuania
Printing and binding: CPI books GmbH, Leck

www.degruyter.com

"For Setsu."

–Alfred Essa

"To my mom, dad and brother."

–Shirin Mojarad

Acknowledgments

AI is a team sport. We would like to thank our former data science team members at McGraw Hill Education for their inspiration and for making us better data scientists: Ani Aghababyan, Lalitha Agnihotri, Jacqueline Feild, Nicholas Lewkow, Mark Riedesel, and Neil Zimmerman.

https://doi.org/10.1515/9781501505737-201

Contents

Part IV: Deep Learning

Preface

There are many books available about artificial intelligence (AI) and machine learning. Ours is a technical work aimed at a non-technical audience. We have written the book primarily for business leaders, managers, and entrepreneurs. But it is intended for anyone responsible, or likely to be responsible, for leading AI-related initiatives in their organization. Our goal is to provide a solid technical foundation for applying AI to solve business problems, old and new. We hope that the book will also be of interest to students as an introductory guide; to practitioners who need to review foundational topics; and to citizens who need to assess the ethical implications of AI.

Why Is AI Important?

There is a broad consensus among economists that AI is not just another technology, but a general purpose technology (GPT) like the steam engine, electricity, and the computer. GPTs are engines of growth: they are pervasive, improve over time, and lead to complementary innovations. As a GPT, AI is poised to drive innovation in every sector of the national and global economy for the foreseeable future. But economists have also cautioned that the full potential of a GPT, including AI, can only be unlocked when firms find new ways to *integrate* culture, business, and technology. AI is important because firms led by AI-savvy business leaders will drive the next wave of innovation and seize competitive advantage in the new economy. AI also introduces deep ethical challenges. To seize the opportunities and to meet the challenges, leaders will need to develop a sound technical understanding of how AI works but also recognize its inherent limitations.

How Is This Book Organized?

Each major topic is presented in three separate chapters: concept, theory, and practice. The concept chapters introduce core concepts with the aim of building a solid intuition. We take a direct route to the topic at hand, without fuss and without too much detail. Each concept chapter contains a case study to emphasize the book's practical nature.

The theory chapter peeks underneath the hood to reveal the machinery behind the concepts. Mathematics is unavoidable, but it need not be forbidding. The power of AI is based on the new science of computation. And the power of computational AI is based on linear algebra and the power of vectors and matrices. The theory chapters, therefore, are also meant to provide a gentle introduction to computational thinking.

The practice chapters provide code in Python to implement the models discussed in the case studies. The code is real code with real examples. Most of the models we

https://doi.org/10.1515/9781501505737-202

discuss can be implemented in 10–20 lines of Python code. This is not to suggest that production-ready code is simple or easy. Far from it. But our approach to coding is to get to the essence of building AI models. The habit of thinking in terms of models develops by viewing and running code in its simplest possible form.

Our coverage of deep learning is organized somewhat differently. We emphasize five foundational principles, dedicating a chapter to each. As before, a practice chapter with code is provided to reinforce key topics.

We have dedicated an entire part of the book, consisting of three chapters to model assessment. The first chapter emphasizes the inherent tradeoff in model development between reducing model error and increasing model generality, the bias-variance tradeoff. The second chapter is dedicated to assessing regression models and the third chapter to assessing classification models.

What Do I Need to Know to Be Able to Understand This Book?

We assume familiarity with college algebra and a nodding familiarity with trigonometry. But more important is a willingness to wade into the waters of abstract thinking. Mastery takes time, patience, and practice. But the rewards of AI, as a system of thought and practice, are well worth knowing and mastering.

What Is Not in This Book?

Our goal has been to highlight key ideas and foundational principles. AI is a vast field and we have not tried to be exhaustive in our coverage. For example, our discussion of deep learning focuses on the core, leaving out specific varieties such as convolutional and recurrent neural networks. We have also left out topics such as dimensionality reduction (e. g., Principal Component Analysis), which is part of unsupervised learning. Our aim is to provide a strong base so that the reader can pursue specialized topics as needed with confidence.

How Should I Read This Book?

Each chapter begins with a list of *key ideas*. The key ideas are meant to serve as landmarks. After finishing each chapter, the reader should return to the list as a diagnostic for comprehension and further study. The code examples in the practice chapters should also be studied in light of the key ideas.

Where Can I Access the Code Examples?

The code examples and the dataset are all available at the book's website: http://practical-ai.org. The Jupyter notebooks can be run directly on the cloud or downloaded from GitHub. Instructions for both are available on the website. The authors maintain two versions of the notebooks. The *quick version* matches the code in the book. The *extended version* includes additional code, with elaboration and further examples, for readers who wish to do a deeper dive into the topics covered in the book.

1 Introduction

In the introduction, we briefly describe the history of AI research: the key distinction is between *general* and *narrow AI*. We then define machine learning, a form of narrow AI. The book's focus is machine learning and deep learning, both are subbranches of narrow AI. We conclude by sketching the basic steps of building machine learning and deep learning models.

1.1 Artificial Intelligence

The dream of artificial intelligence goes back centuries. Its connection to computing was articulated most clearly by the German mathematician and philosopher Gottfried Wilhelm Leibniz (Figure 1.1), a co-inventor of calculus with Sir Isaac Newton. In 1666, Leibniz published *On the Combinatorial Art*, in which he postulated that all human thought rests on atomic concepts; that these atomic concepts can be represented symbolically; and that compound concepts can be generated combinatorially with automated rules.

Figure 1.1: Gottfried Wilhelm Leibniz (1646–1716). Painting by Christoph Bernhard Francke. Wikicommons. Creative Commons Licence CC0.

Leibniz also imagined a *machine* which he called "the great instrument of reason." Leibniz's machine would be based on three things: an "alphabet of human thoughts" represented symbolically in a formal language; a set of logical rules for combining and recombining the alphabet; and the mechanical device itself, which could carry out the operations of combination and recombination.

Leibniz postulated that if we had such a universal logical machine, it would be able to answer all questions and resolve all disputes. "When there are disputes among persons," Leibniz wrote, "we can simply say, 'Let us calculate,' and without further ado, see who is right."

https://doi.org/10.1515/9781501505737-001

Leibniz's machine embodies Spock-like logic. It knows nothing of experience. Perhaps the earliest statement of artificial intelligence which connects machines to experience comes from the founder of modern computer science, Alan Turing (Figure 1.2). In a public lecture given in 1947, Turing conceived of a computing machine that *learns* from experience: "What we want is a machine that can learn from experience," and that the "possibility of letting the machine alter its own instructions proves the mechanism for this." In founding computer science, Turing also showed that there are inherent limits to computation and, therefore, limits to what machines can achieve. Leibniz's ambitious dream of a universal logical machine is not realizable, in principle. But machines can achieve great things, within limits and under the active guidance of humans.

Figure 1.2: Alan Turing (1912–1954). Wikicommons. Creative Commons Licence CC0.

Modern AI research began in the mid-1950s. Herbert Simon, an AI pioneer, wrote in 1965 that "machines will be capable, within twenty years, of doing any work a man can do." Let's call this *general AI*, the hypothetical ability of machines to learn and perform any intellectual task that a human being can. Despite Simon's prediction, general AI remains elusive to this day.

By contrast, progress in *narrow AI* has been rapid in recent years. By narrow AI we mean the use of machines to solve *particular* tasks. Examples of narrow AI include:
- Facial-recognition software
- Google's page-ranking algorithm powering their search engine
- Recommendation systems for music listening and movie viewing
- Automated email spam filtering
- Navigation systems on the Mars rover and its helicopter
- Credit card fraud detection algorithms
- Algorithms for detecting gravitational waves

The list grows each day. Narrow AI is accelerating for several reasons. First, narrow AI has led to an unprecedented automation of human tasks. AI is automating not just routine tasks, but also tasks previously thought to be beyond the reach of computers. Second, narrow AI is often able to outperform humans for certain tasks. Third, AI relies heavily on computation, and the cost of computation continues to decline. Finally, as a GPT, AI has a spillover effect in generating innovations and new business models.

1.2 What Is Machine Learning?

The basis of narrow AI is machine learning. What is machine learning? The best definition comes from Arthur Samuel, a pioneer in the field of artificial intelligence. Samuel defined machine learning as the "field of study that gives computers the ability to learn without being explicitly programmed."

Let's unpack the definition by contrasting machine learning with traditional programming. We need some task to be performed, and we want the computer to perform the task. In traditional programming (Figure 1.3), the computer is given the data and the program as inputs. From the data and the program, the computer then produces an output.

Traditional Programming

Figure 1.3: In traditional programming, the program is an input. The program is typically written by humans.

In this scheme, the program is an explicit set of instructions, also called an *algorithm*. The algorithm can be thought of as a recipe: a set of rules for transforming the data into the desired output. In traditional programming the program is written explicitly by humans. The program also remains fixed unless humans intervene and rewrite the rules.

Now let's look at machine learning. In machine learning (Figure 1.4), the computer is given the data and the desired output for a given task. From the data and the output, the computer produces the program. The desired output is also called the label.

Machine Learning

Figure 1.4: In machine learning, the machine "learns" the program from the data and the labeled output.

The program is said to be "learned" by the computer. It is not written by humans. Moreover, the program can evolve and improve based on experience, as the computer is fed new data and new outputs.

From a mathematical perspective, in traditional programming the computer is provided with an input X and a function $f()$. The function is in the form of a program written by humans. The computer then computes an output y based on $f(X)$. In machine learning, the computer is provided with input X and an output y from which it produces a function $f()$, a set of rules which map X to y. This contrast in the role of functions is shown in Figure 1.5.

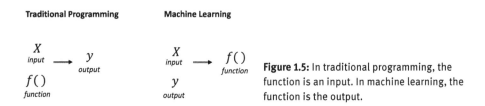

Figure 1.5: In traditional programming, the function is an input. In machine learning, the function is the output.

Why do we need machine learning? What justifies its elevation to a General Purpose Technology (GPT)? In traditional programming, a programmer or a team of programmers *explicitly* write a program to carry out a task. But it turns out that for a large number of tasks writing an explicit program is either impractical or impossible. Many of the tasks performed by humans is based on tacit knowledge. For example, we can easily and quickly separate pictures of cats from pictures of dogs. Writing a computer program to do the same task with a high degree of accuracy is nearly impossible. By contrast, a computer using machine learning can perform the task quickly and with astonishing accuracy.

1.3 Areas of Machine Learning

In general, there are three types of machine learning: *supervised learning*, *unsupervised learning*, and *reinforcement learning*.

Supervised learning is the characteristic form of machine learning described above. A computer is given sample inputs and desired outputs. The computer's goal in machine learning is to figure out the rule or function that maps inputs to outputs.

In *Unsupervised Learning* (also called data mining) there are no outputs or labels. The computer tries to discover structure or patterns hidden in the data. The most widely used example of unsupervised learning is *clustering*, where the computer tries to detect groups in the data. Another form of unsupervised learning is dimensionality reduction, where the computer takes a high-dimensional dataset and reduces it to a smaller, more manageable set of dimensions.

In *Reinforcement Learning* a computer interacts with a changing environment in which it must attain a goal, such as driving a car or winning a game. The computer receives feedback in terms of rewards and punishments as it navigates towards the goal.

Deep Learning is a subset of machine learning. It is based on neural networks and among its advantages is the ability to "learn" extremely difficult programs with very large datasets.

The primary focus of the book is supervised machine learning. The essence of supervised learning is *prediction*. Through narrow AI, machines can predict faster, cheaper, and better – all at scale. Indeed, any task that involves prediction is ripe for business disruption.

1.4 Machine Learning Workflow

Throughout the book, we will emphasize five steps (Figure 1.6) as part of the machine learning workflow. The steps are not always linear. They are also not one-time, but iterative.

The first step is to define and prepare the data. In making predictions, for example, we have to identify the target of prediction (target variable) and the data used to make the predictions (feature variables). Very often the data needs to be cleansed and transformed before we can build machine learning models.

During the second step, we identify a *model type*. There are a variety of model types, including multiple linear regression, logistic regression, and deep learning. The model types we discuss are meant to be illustrative, not comprehensive. We review the most important types to build a strong foundation.

Figure 1.6: The machine learning workflow consists of five major steps.

During the third step, we *fit* the model type to the data. The model type can be thought of as a template. Fitting the model to the data generates the specific model for the data. The specific model is the rule, function or program described above. This is also the step in which the machine "learns" the algorithm.

During the fourth step, we *evaluate* the model for accuracy. Depending on the model type and the application, there are a variety of metrics that can be used to evaluate the accuracy of the specific model. We will see, for example, that the metrics for evaluating regression are very different from those for classification.

Finally, we use the model to predict new data. The hallmark of machine learning and deep learning is prediction of new data. During training, the machine learning algorithm learns the correct model for the data, and then uses the model to predict unseen data.

Part I: **Machine Learning I**

2 Simple Linear Regression – Concept

In this chapter, we begin our study of machine learning with simple linear regression (SLR). Despite its simplicity, linear regression is among the most powerful techniques in the AI practitioner's toolkit. A solid grasp of its core concepts is also essential for tackling more advanced methods such as deep learning.

> **Key Idea 1.** In simple linear regression (SLR), a *single* feature variable is used to predict a *single* target variable.
>
> **Key Idea 2.** In SLR, the feature and target variables are both *continuous*.
>
> **Key Idea 3.** In SLR, the model takes the form a *straight line*, also called the *regression line* and the *line of best fit*.
>
> **Key Idea 4.** A regression model is uniquely specified by its *parameters*. SLR has two model parameters: β_0 and β_1. β_0 is the intercept of the regression line and β_1 is the slope.
>
> **Key Idea 5.** In SLR, two key metrics are used to evaluate *model performance*: Mean Squared Error (MSE) and R^2 (pronounced "R squared").

2.1 Bird's Eye View

As indicated in the Introduction, model development in supervised machine learning consists of five basic steps. First, we prepare a dataset and perform basic descriptive analysis. Second, we choose a model type. Third, we fit the model type to the data. In the process, the machine learning algorithm "learns" the parameters of the model. Fourth, we evaluate the performance of the model. Finally, we use the model to predict new data.

In all supervised machine learning, the pattern is the same. We go from data to model and then from model to prediction of new data. The model is a bridge (Figure 2.1), allowing us to go from existing data to new data. Let's look at each step in more detail for simple linear regression.

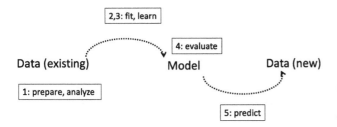

Figure 2.1: Model development workflow consists of five major steps.

https://doi.org/10.1515/9781501505737-002

Step 1

Our starting point is a dataset. In SLR, the dataset can be represented as a table of two columns, as shown in Table 2.1. Each row in the table is an observation, record, or example. By convention, we use y to represent the target variable and x to represent the feature variable. The target variable is the data we are trying to predict. The feature variable is the data we use to make the prediction. In mathematics, x is referred to as the *independent* variable and y is the *dependent* variable. In statistics, x is called the *predictor* or *regressor* variable and y is the *response* variable.

Table 2.1: SLR data can be represented as a two-dimensional table. The first column is the feature variable. The second column is the target variable.

x	y
2.1	60.5
4.5	133.0
2.7	72.8
32.4	96.9
2.8	112.3

For smaller datasets, a two-dimensional dataset can be visualized with a scatterplot, as shown in Figure 2.2. In the scatterplot, the x-axis is the feature variable and the y-axis is the target variable.

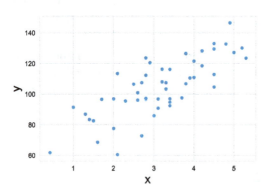

Figure 2.2: A scatterplot with the feature variable on the x-axis and the target variable on the y-axis.

Thus far, we have specified how data is represented in SLR. Step 1 also includes preparing the data and performing basic descriptive analysis. Once these are done, we can move on to Step 2.

Step 2

Given a prepared dataset, the next step is to find a *model type*. SLR is only one among many model types in machine learning. In later chapters, we will introduce other model types. For now, let's assume we have chosen SLR as our model type.

Step 3

Once we choose SLR as our model type, the SLR algorithm takes over. The algorithm considers various straight lines as candidate models, as shown in Figure 2.3. The number of specific models to choose from is infinite since there are an infinite number of straight lines in a two-dimensional plane.

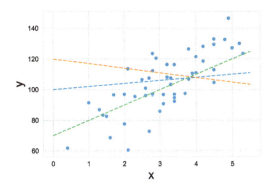

Figure 2.3: The figure shows three lines, but all lines in the plane are candidate models.

Among the infinite set of candidate lines, only one line is the line of best fit. The SLR algorithm discovers the unique line of best fit, as shown in Figure 2.4. What characterizes the line of best fit? Intuitively, the line of best fit is the unique straight line *closest* to the given data points. We will examine the concept of closeness systematically in the next chapter. For now, we will accept that the SLR algorithm correctly discovers the unique straight line of best fit. The line of best fit is also called the *regression line*.

For our example dataset, the regression line turns out to have a slope of 12.8 and an intercept of 64.0, as shown in Figure 2.4. Since a straight line is uniquely characterized by its slope and intercept, the equation of the regression line for our example dataset can be written as: $y = 12.8x + 64.0$.

Step 4

Once we have a model or regression line, we need to evaluate the model for accuracy. In regression, the two central metrics for evaluating models are Mean Squared Error

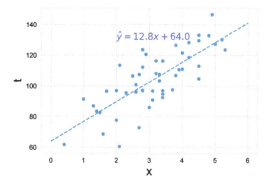

Figure 2.4: The regression line is the "line of best fit," the unique line that is closest to the data points.

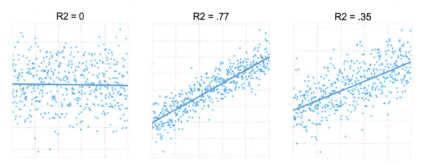

Figure 2.5: Three examples of R^2. The left panel ($R^2 = 0$) is a very poor fit. The middle panel ($R^2 = .77$) is an excellent fit. The right panel ($R^2 = .35$) is a poor to good fit, depending on the domain and context.

(MSE) and R^2 (pronounced "R squared"). We examine both in detail in later chapters. For now, we make some initial observations about the two concepts.

In Step 2, we said that the regression line, or the line of best fit, is the unique line which is *closest* to the set of data points. We can express the same point by stating that the line of best fit is the one which has the least error. If we think of shooting a set of arrows at a target, the most accurate arrow is also the one with the least error. MSE is a way of quantifying the error in our models. Among all the lines in the plane, the regression line is the line for which MSE is the least.

What about R^2? Why do we need it? MSE is useful for comparing two different models against the same dataset. The regression line is guaranteed to have a lower MSE than all other lines in the plane. But the specific value of MSE depends on the units of the target variable and the specific dataset. For comparing models across different datasets and variables with different units, we need a metric other than MSE.

R^2 as a metric for comparing models is independent of the unit of measurement. It is always a number between 0 to 1. At the extremes, a model with $R^2 = 0$ is a very poor fit and a model with $R^2 = 1$ is a perfect fit. For our example, R^2 for the model turns out to have the value of .59, which is a moderate fit. We add the caution, however, that determining "goodness of fit" is entirely dependent on the domain and the context of the problem being solved.

Figure 2.5 shows three examples of R^2. Each example consists of a dataset, the corresponding regression line discovered by SLR, and the corresponding value for R^2. The first example (left panel) has an R^2 close to 0, which means that there is essentially no relationship between the feature (x-axis) and target variable (y-axis). The example illustrates the fact that merely having a regression line doesn't guarantee that the model is a good fit.

In the second example (middle panel), the value for R^2 is .77, which is moderate to high. From the scatterplot, we can also see that data points hug the regression line quite closely. The model seems to be a good fit.

In the third example (right panel), the value for R^2 is .35. Depending on the context, the regression line in the third example might not be a good model. We discuss R^2 in detail in Chapter 9.

Step 5

Once we have a model (i. e., the regression line) for the dataset, we can use it to predict y for new values of x. We can predict new y values simply by plugging in the value for x in the regression line's equation:

$$y = 12.8 \times \mathbf{5.5} + 64 = 134.6$$

Figure 2.6 displays the predicted values for three new points not in our original dataset. It should be noted that all predicted values fall on the regression line.

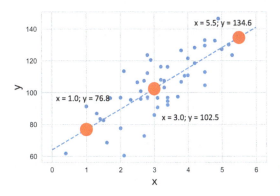

Figure 2.6: We use the regression line to predict new data.

In summary, in SLR we begin with a set of points (x, y). The machine learning algorithm fits a straight line, called the regression line, to the data. We evaluate the fitted model for accuracy. Finally, the regression line is then used to predict new data.

2.2 Fundamental Equation of SLR

Machine learning is applied mathematics. If mathematical results are viewed as a series of peaks in a mountain range, then notation is among the mathematical mountaineer's most important tools. As we proceed, we will also develop our knowledge of mathematical notation. In this section, we continue with our knowledge of mathematical notation for machine learning and build toward stating the Fundamental Equation of SLR.

Mathematical notation

In SLR, we use a single variable **x** to predict another single variable **y**.

$$x \xrightarrow{\text{predicts}} y$$

Mathematically, this means finding a function f such that given some input x, we get an output y:

$$y = f(x)$$

It is useful to think of a function as performing a series of operations on an input x to produce an output y. In SLR, the operation is given by the familiar equation of a straight line:

$$y = mx + b$$

The function for a straight line takes the input x, multiplies it by a constant m ("slope"), and then adds the constant b ("intercept") to the previous result. In machine learning, it is customary to use the Greek letter β (pronounced "beta") with subscripts, rather than m and b to represent the slope and intercept. Accordingly, we rewrite the equation of a straight line as:

$$\text{SLR Fundamental Equation:} \quad y = \beta_0 + \beta_1 x \qquad (2.1)$$

Equation (2.1) is the Fundamental Equation of Simple Linear Regression. The equation represents a straight line with an intercept of β_0 and a slope of β_1. In SLR, fitting a model to the data means finding the specific values for β_0 and β_1. β_0 and β_1 are also called the *parameters* of the model.

Models and Errors

All models are approximations. This fundamental fact requires us to make an important adjustment in our notation. The relation of data to model can be expressed with a simple conceptual equation:

$$\text{DATA} = \text{MODEL} + \text{ERROR}$$

DATA stands for our historical dataset. The starting dataset in supervised learning is also referred to as the "ground truth." **MODEL** stands for the machine learning model that is learned against the data. No matter how accurate the model, there will always be some error. **ERROR** stands for the discrepancy between the ground truth in the data compared to the model.

The conceptual equation can be rewritten formally as:

$$y = \hat{y} + \epsilon$$

In the equation, y stands for DATA (the actual values of the target variable in our dataset), $\hat{y}$ stands for MODEL (values for the same x as predicted by our model), and ϵ stands for ERROR (the difference between the actual values and the model's prediction).

Incorporating the notion of error, we can rewrite the fundamental equation as:

$$\text{SLR Fundamental Equation:} \quad y = \hat{\beta}_0 + \hat{\beta}_1 x + \epsilon \tag{2.2}$$

Whenever we see the "hat" symbol over a variable or constant, it should be read as indicating an estimate. We can state then that the goal of model development is to *estimate* a function $\hat{y}$ which minimizes the error ϵ. A perfect model, never attainable in practice, is one in which the error is 0, and therefore: $y = \hat{y}$.

2.3 Some Assumptions of Simple Linear Regression

We have said that the primary aim of supervised machine learning is prediction. We begin with a dataset. We use machine learning to find a model for the dataset. We then use the model to predict new data. But how do we know which method to use? How do we know that SLR is the correct model type for the data at hand?

Unfortunately, there is no single true and tested method for finding the most appropriate model type. But before choosing any particular model type, it's good practice to understand and review the model type's assumptions. In this section, we state some assumptions of SLR. The list is not comprehensive. But it can be used as a preliminary checklist when considering whether SLR is the appropriate model type.

SLR has a single feature variable

SLR's first assumption is that we use only a *single* variable (x) to make predictions. In later chapters, we will learn to use multiple variables. Simple Linear Regression is called "simple" because it uses only *one* variable to make predictions.

$$x \xrightarrow{\text{predicts}} y$$

What are some examples of SLR? We might wish to predict personal income based solely on years of education; the price of a house based solely on total square feet; expected revenue for a product based solely on advertising spend; or, a student's exam grade based solely on hours of sleep the night before.

Feature and target variables are continuous

SLR's second assumption is that both the feature and target variables are *continuous*. In machine learning we typically deal with two types of numerical variables: *continuous* and *discrete*. A variable that can assume *any* real number value between two given values is continuous; otherwise, it is discrete. A person's height, for example, is a continuous variable. The result of a throwing a six-sided diced is discrete, since there are only six possible outcomes.

What about categorical variables or non-numerical variables? We will see in subsequent chapters that for machine learning, categories have to be transformed into discrete numerical variables.

Relationship between feature and target variable is not-random

SLR's third assumption is that feature and target variables are *related*. In other words, we assume that the co-occurrence of the two variables is not due to chance. Not everything in the world is related. Shoe sales on a particular day and time in Barcelona, Spain is not likely to be related to ice cream sales on the same day and time in Osaka, Japan.

How can we tell if two variables are related? There is no definitive test. However, statistics comes to the rescue by allowing us to sift genuine relationship from spurious ones. In the course of the book, we learn to apply some simple statistical tests to evaluate the relationship between input and output variables. Two important statistical tests are correlation and hypothesis testing.

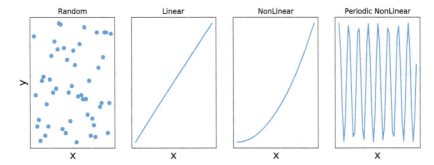

Figure 2.7: Some possible relationships among the variables x and y.

Relationship between feature and target variable is approximately linear

SLR's fourth assumption states that feature and target variables are not only related but that the specific form of the relationship is *linear* or can be approximated by a linear function.

Given two variables there are a variety of possible relationships. In the first panel of Figure 2.7, it's likely that there is no relationship between the variables x and y. In the second panel, the relationship is linear. As x increases, so does y. Moreover, the *rate of increase*, or the slope of the line is constant throughout the curve. In the third panel, the relationship is non-linear. As x increases, so does y. However, the rate of increase also increases. In the fourth panel, the relationship is non-linear and periodic. The slope increases in some parts of the curve, decreases in other parts, and is sometimes zero. The same pattern recurs throughout the graph.

In summary, when we apply SLR to a set of data points we assume that we are able to predict some variable y with only a single variable x; that both x and y are continuous variables; that the two variables co-occurrence is not random; and, finally, that the two variables can be modeled linearly. These are some baseline assumptions for SLR. There are additional assumptions for regression, which we review in later chapters.

2.4 Case Study: Is Earning Related to Learning?

Having gained a basic overview of SLR, we are ready to apply our knowledge with a case study. Analytics, including machine learning, begins with well-formulated questions. Our case study poses the following question: *Is learning related to earning?* In other words, do educated people earn more? If so, can we model the relationship of education to income? Can we predict someone's income knowing their level of education?

Dataset

The dataset contains 35 rows or observations. Each row is a unique person. Table 2.2 displays sample entries. The table contains two columns: *Education* level, in units of years of education, and *Income*, in units of thousands of dollars. Both variables are continuous.

Table 2.2: Sample data. *Education* is the feature variable. *Income* is the target variable for the regression.

Education	Income
10.0	32.1
10.4	36.5
10.7	23.9
11.1	52.3
11.4	30.2

Exploratory Data Analysis

Model development should always be preceded by exploratory data analysis. Table 2.3 provides elementary summary statistics of the dataset. The dataset contains 35 observations. The mean and standard deviation for the variable *Education* are 16 and 3.6, respectively. For *Income*, the mean and standard deviation are 66.0 and 21.5, respectively.

Table 2.3: Summary statistics for *Education* and *Income*.

Statistic	Education	Income
count	35	35
mean	16.0	66.0
std	3.6	21.5
min	10.0	23.9
50 %	16.0	67.7
max	22.0	110.8

A scatterplot can be an excellent way to visualize two-dimensional data. A visual inspection in Figure 2.8 shows that the relationship between *Education* and *Income* seems to be linear. As *Education* increases, so does *Income*. The rate of increase also seems to be constant.

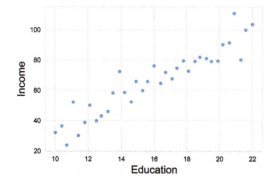

Figure 2.8: A scatterplot of *Education* vs. *Income* indicates that the relationship is likely to be linear.

A correlation of the two variables *Education* and *Income* yields a value of .9, which suggests that there is a strong relationship between the two variables.

In summary, our preliminary Exploratory Data Analysis indicates that an SLR model for the dataset seems promising and appropriate.

Performing regression

We are now ready to apply Simple Linear Regression to our dataset. In the Practice chapter for SLR, we will learn to use Python to perform regression. Applying regression to the dataset yields the regression line shown in Figure 2.9. The regression line has a slope (β_1 = 5.6) and an intercept (β_0 = −23.2).

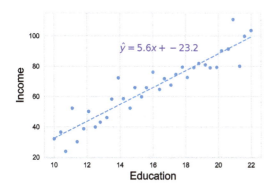

Figure 2.9: The regression yields the line $\hat{y}$ = 5.6x − 23.2.

Recall that the regression equation for SLR is:

$$\hat{y} = \hat{\beta}_0 + \hat{\beta}_1 x$$

Given the results of the regression we can write the equation as:

$$\widehat{Income} = -23.2 + 5.6 \times Education$$

Making predictions

Given the regression line, we are now in a position to make predictions. Suppose we wish to predict income for three hypothetical students, each with a different level of schooling: a high school graduate (12 years of education); a college graduate (16 years of education); and a master's degree student (18 years of education).

The predictions can be made easily using the regression equation. We plug in the value for x and calculate the corresponding value of y based on the regression equation.

$$Income \text{ (high school degree)} = -23.2 + 5.6 \times \mathbf{12} = 44.0$$
$$Income \text{ (bachelor's degree)} = -23.2 + 5.6 \times \mathbf{16} = 66.4$$
$$Income \text{ (master's degree)} = -23.2 + 5.6 \times \mathbf{18} = 77.6$$

We can also plot the predictions against the scatterplot (see Figure 2.10) of the original data. We note again that all predictions of income based on education fall on the regression line.

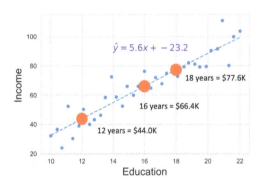

Figure 2.10: We use the regression line to predict income for 12 years, 16 years, and 18 years of education.

2.5 Interpreting Regression

Models should predict accurately. But models should also be understandable by humans. In our study of machine learning, we will see that regression models have an important advantage over other approaches. They are simpler, but they are also interpretable.

Before we tackle how to interpret an SLR model, let's consider what we might mean more generally by "interpretability." Machine learning models are mathematical functions. A mathematical function can be viewed as a box. The box accepts a set of numbers as input and produces a set of numbers as output.

When we care about interpretability, we care about what happens *inside* the box. The box accepts some input and applies a series of *transformations* or operations to produce the output. We can visualize the transformations as a set of mechanical gears turning inside the box. In the language of machine learning the gears are the *parameters* of the model. Now we are ready to state a working definition of an interpretable model.

In the case of an interpretable model, we know the *number* of gears inside the box, their *arrangement*, and how *each gear* in the sequence influences the output.

Let's look now at an SLR model using our definition of interpretability. An SLR model, as shown in Figure 2.11, has exactly two gears or parameters: the intercept β_0 and the slope β_1.

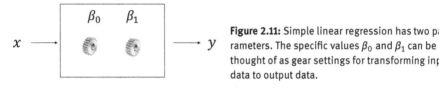

Figure 2.11: Simple linear regression has two parameters. The specific values β_0 and β_1 can be thought of as gear settings for transforming input data to output data.

The sequence of transformations inside the box is clear. We accept some input x, multiply it by the constant β_1 and then add the constant β_0 to the result. In our case study, the gears are set at $\beta_0 = -23.2$ and $\beta_1 = 5.6$.

Now we are ready to interpret SLR. Let's begin with the slope. In a regression model, the slope β_1 tells us that a *one-unit increase* in x leads to β_1 increase in y. In our case study, this means that one year of education leads approximately to an increase of $5,600 in income. What is the difference in income between a high school and a college graduate? The difference in education between the two students is four years. We can calculate the difference in income between them by multiplying the slope ($\beta_1 = 5.6 \times 4$), which yields 22.4, or a $22,400 dollar increase in yearly income.

We have to be more careful about interpreting the intercept. The intercept (value of β_0) yields the value of y when $x = 0$. In our case study, the literal interpretation is that someone with 0 years of education can expect a negative income of –$23,200. This, of course, makes no sense. One way to attach sense to the intercept is to constrain the model to certain bounds or range, in the x-axis. In our case study, we might stipulate that the model is applicable only for the values ranging from 8 to 20, meaning 8 to 20 years of education.

2.6 Summary

In this chapter, we introduced SLR as a basic model for machine learning. In SLR, we use a single feature variable to predict a single target variable. The model in SLR is a straight line, called the regression line. We then reviewed some fundamental assumptions of SLR. We also saw that an SLR model is highly interpretable. One unit of change in the feature variable predicts a change of β_1 units (i. e., slope of the regression line) in the target variable. The value of the intercept (β_0) tells us the value of the target variable when the feature variable is 0. But we noted that in SLR intercepts have to be interpreted with caution, depending on the dataset.

3 Simple Linear Regression – Theory

In the last chapter, we introduced Simple Linear Regression (SLR) as modeling the relationship between two continuous variables. The model takes the form of a straight line of best fit, also called the regression line. Intuitively, the line of best fit is the line closest to a given set of points. In this chapter, we define precisely what is meant by the line of best fit.

Key Idea 1. In SLR, the regression line is the unique straight line closest to a given set of points in a two-dimensional plane.

Key Idea 2. Machine learning employs a variety of distance metrics. A distance metric is a method for measuring the distance between two entities. The most common distance metric is Euclidean distance from basic geometry.

Key Idea 3. SLR uses a distance metric which involves squaring the residuals. A residual is the same as error: the gap between the actual value (y) and the predicted value ($\hat{y}$).

Key Idea 4. In SLR, the regression line is the unique line which *minimizes* the sum of the squares of the residuals or error terms.

Key Idea 5. In SLR, the regression line can be discovered either analytically or numerically.

3.1 Some Basics of Measuring Distance

In the previous chapter, we stated that the line of best fit, the regression line, is the one that is closest to a set of data points. But how is closeness defined? Measuring closeness means being able to measure distance.

In this chapter, we begin by reviewing how to calculate distances using familiar Euclidean geometry: the distance between two points; the distance between a line and a point; and, finally, the distance between a line and a set of points.

Once we are able to calculate the distance between a line and a set of points, we can pose an initial criterion for the line of best fit. The initial criterion involves calculating Total Absolute Error (TAE). It turns out though that this initial criterion is *not* adequate for regression. We have to adjust the initial criterion slightly. Once we do so, we arrive at the criterion for determining the line of best fit in regression: Residual Sum of Squares (RSS).

Distance between two points

We begin by reviewing the concept of measuring the distance between two points. From basic geometry we can calculate the distance between two points **a** and **b** by applying the Pythagorean Theorem.

https://doi.org/10.1515/9781501505737-003

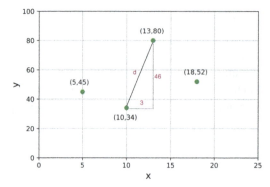

Figure 3.1: Distance between two points is calculated using the Pythagorean Theorem.

If $\mathbf{a} = (x_1, y_1)$ and $\mathbf{b} = (x_2, y_2)$, then the distance d between the two points is simply:

$$d = \sqrt{(x_1 - x_2)^2 + (y_1 - y_2)^2}$$

For example, the distance between the points $(13, 80)$ and $(10, 34)$ is shown in Figure 3.1:

$$d = \sqrt{(13 - 10)^2 + (80 - 34)^2} = 46.1$$

Distance from a line to a single point

Next, we consider how to compute the distance from a line to a single point. Figure 3.2 shows a line and a point. The point has the coordinates $(13, 80)$. The line's equation is: $y = 3x + 20$.

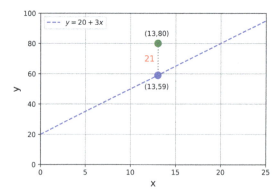

Figure 3.2: The distance between a line and a point is the vertical distance from the point to the line.

The distance between a single point and a line is defined as the *vertical distance* from the point to the line. Imagine a plumb line descending vertically from the point to the line. In Figure 3.2, the coordinate of the single point is (13, 80). The coordinate of the corresponding point (i. e., same *x-coordinate*) on the line is (13, 59). Therefore, the vertical distance of the point to the line is 80 − 59 = 21.

Residual

In the context of regression, we will speak of the distance between a point and a line as a *residual*. Notationally, we will use y to represent the data point, $\hat{y}$ to represent the corresponding data point (i. e., same x-coordinate) on the line, and the Greek letter ϵ (epsilon) to represent the residual. The residual, as the distance between a point and a line, is shown in Figure 3.3.

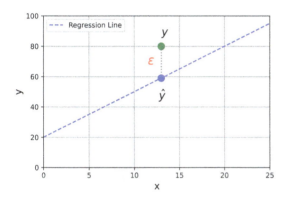

Figure 3.3: The residual or error is the distance of a point to a line.

The residual is then calculated as:

$$\epsilon = y - \hat{y}$$

More generally, the residual of the ith point can be written as:

$$\epsilon_i = y_i - \hat{y}_i$$

In the previous chapter, we encountered the same formula in relating data to model and error, except we used the term "error" instead of "residual." But error and residual are equivalent concepts: both represent the discrepancy of a model to the ground truth.

Distance from a line to a set of points

We are now ready to define the distance from a line to a set of points. We define the distance between the line and a set of points as the sum of the absolute values of the residuals. In other words, we calculate the residual of each data point, take its absolute value, and then sum the results. Using indices and the summation convention, we can write the sum of the absolute value of the residuals as:

$$\sum_{i=1}^{n} |\epsilon_i| = \sum_{i=1}^{n} |y_i - \hat{y}_i|$$

Why absolute value? We sum the absolute value of the residuals to ensure that the total sum is always positive. Otherwise, the distances of the points to the line will cancel each other out.

Let's consider an example. Suppose we have four points and a line, as shown in the left panel of Figure 3.4. To calculate the distance of the four points to the line, we calculate the corresponding residuals of the four points as shown in the right panel of Figure 3.4.

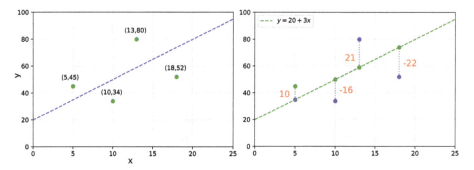

Figure 3.4: Distance from a line to a set of points is the sum of the absolute values of the vertical distances.

The distance of the line to the set of points is calculated then as the sum of the absolute values of the residuals:

$$\sum_{i=1}^{n} |\epsilon_i| = |10| + |-16| + |21| + |-22| = 49$$

3.2 Total Absolute Error (TAE)

Armed with the definition of distance between a line and a set of points as the sum of the absolute value of the residuals, we are now ready to state a criterion for determining the line of best fit.

We first name the sum of the absolute residuals as the Total Absolute Error (TAE).

$$\overline{TAE} \equiv \sum_{i=1}^{n} |\epsilon_i| = \sum_{i=1}^{n} |y_i - \hat{y}_i| \qquad (3.1)$$

We can now state a possible criterion for the line of best fit. The line of best fit is the unique line for which TAE is the least.

According to this criterion, we compare various lines in the plane by calculating their TAE. We then select the line whose TAE is the least. TAE is a perfectly good criterion for identifying the line of best fit. But it turns out that in regression, it is not the *preferred* criterion. The reasons for this are technical. For the curious, a hint lies in why statistics squares distances when measuring the spread (e. g., variance or standard deviation) for a set of points.

Taking our cue from statistics, we modify our criterion slightly to arrive at the criterion for the line of best fit as used in regression.

3.3 Residual Sum of Squares (RSS)

In regression, instead of taking the sum of absolute errors to calculate the distance between a set of points and a line, we sum instead the squares of the residuals. We call the sum the Residual Sum of Squares (RSS):

$$\overline{RSS} \equiv \sum_{i=1}^{n} \epsilon_i^2 = \sum_{i=1}^{n} (y_i - \hat{y}_i)^2 \qquad (3.2)$$

Let's consider an example. Suppose we are given two lines and a set of points, as in Figure 3.5. We calculate the distance of each line to the set points using RSS. We then compare to see which line has a smaller RSS.

Table 3.1 provides the numerical calculations of RSS for the two lines. The RSS for line 1 is 581 and for line 2 it is 241. Since RSS for line 2 is smaller than for line 1, we conclude that line 2 is closer to the data points.

Table 3.1: Calculating RSS for two lines.

x	y	$\hat{y}_1$	$\hat{y}_2$	ϵ^2 (line1)	ϵ^2 (line2)
5	40	35	45	25	25
10	34	50	50	36	36
13	65	59	53	36	144
18	52	74	58	484	36
				RSS = 581	RSS = 241

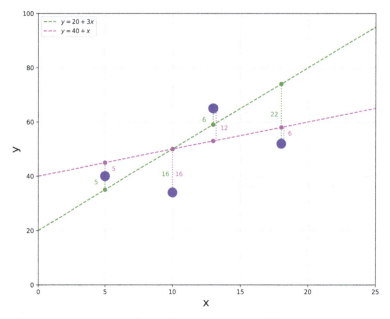

Figure 3.5: We compare RSS for two lines to determine which line is closer to the points.

Given RSS, we are now ready to restate our criterion for the line of best fit in regression:

The line of best fit is the unique line one for which **RSS** is the least.

3.4 Mean Squared Error

We have learned that the line of best fit in regression is one that minimizes the Residual Sum of Squares (RSS). RSS measures the error or discrepancy between actual data and predicted data as generated by the model.

RSS is closely related to another commonly used term for error, namely Mean Squared Error (MSE). MSE is just RSS divided by the number of observations (n) in our data. RSS and MSE differ only by a constant factor. Therefore, they are often used equivalently as a measure of error.

$$\widehat{MSE} = \frac{\text{RSS}}{n}$$

We can also express MSE directly as:

$$\widehat{MSE} = \frac{1}{n}\sum_{i=1}^{n}(y_i - \hat{y}_i)^2 \tag{3.3}$$

For the sake of completeness, we also state another common expression for error, namely Root Mean Squared Error (RMSE). RMSE is merely the square root of MSE.

$$\widehat{RMSE} = \sqrt{\frac{\sum_{i=1}^{n}(y_i - \hat{y}_i)^2}{n}} \tag{3.4}$$

Students of statistics will be sure to have noticed that the formula for MSE is similar in form to the one for variance and RMSE to standard deviation.

3.5 Analytical vs. Numerical Solutions in Machine Learning

RSS is a criterion for the line of best fit. Given two lines, we can compare which is a better fit by calculating their RSS. RSS, however, is not a method or procedure for finding the best line of best fit. The criterion lets us compare two lines to determine which is closer to a set of points. But among the infinite lines in a plane, the criterion does not help us find the unique line that is the closest.

Fortunately, the line of best fit can be estimated from two simple formulas. The slope of the line of best fit is calculated as:

$$\hat{\beta}_1 = \frac{s_y}{s_x}r \tag{3.5}$$

In Formula (3.5), s_y is the standard deviation of the target variable y; s_x is the standard deviation of the feature variable x; and r is the Pearson correlation between x and y.

Once we know the slope for the line of best fit (i. e., β_1), we can derive the intercept from the formula:

$$\hat{\beta}_0 = \bar{y} - \hat{\beta}_1\bar{x} \tag{3.6}$$

In Formula (3.6), $\bar{y}$ is the mean of the target variable and $\bar{x}$ is the mean of feature variable.

Being able to arrive at estimates of machine learning parameters "analytically," as we did above using formulas, is rare. For most applications in machine learning analytical solutions are either impractical or impossible. In machine learning parameters most often are estimated "numerically." We will learn about numerical methods later in our study of *gradient descent* in deep learning.

Fortunately, machine learning algorithms do most of the heavy lifting behind the scenes with numerical estimates. Nonetheless, machine learning practitioners should have a good understanding of how some of the most common numerical solutions work.

3.6 Summary

In simple linear regression, our goal is to estimate the line of best fit for set of data points. The method consists of two steps. First, we define a metric for calculating the distance between a line and a set of points. The metric used in SLR, Residual Sum of Squares, involves summing the squares of the residuals. We also noted that the RSS also defines error, the discrepancy between the observed values of the data and the predictions made by the model. We then stated that the criterion for determining the line of best fit is one that minimizes RSS. Second, we saw that RSS alone does not provide a method for discovering the actual line of best fit. In SLR, an exact analytical solution is available for determining the slope (β_1) and intercept (β_0) for the line of best fit. We also noted that approximate numerical methods can also be used to model parameters. In particular, the method of *gradient descent* will come up in our study of deep learning.

4 Simple Linear Regression – Practice

The case study for simple linear regression tries to answer the question: Is earning related to learning? In other words, does more education lead to higher earnings? As a machine learning task, we will use simple linear regression. Our feature variable is *Education*. Our target variable is *Income*. The code is in Python. Using the code requires basic familiarity with Python, but the programming logic should be accessible to anyone familiar with a basic programming languages.

Python libraries

Python comes with many libraries. A library is a set of useful pre-written functions which eliminate the need to write programs from scratch. The most import library for machine learning in Python is **scikit-learn**. A complementary statistical library is **statsmodels**, which is especially useful for regression models and also contains an extensive list of statistical tests and measures. We will see later that deep learning has is its own set of libraries.

    Pandas is a widely used Python library for data analysis and data manipulation. **Pandas** makes use of **numpy**, the fundamental library in Python for numeric and scientific computation. As part of the machine learning workflow, it is common to perform the initial stages of data cleansing and analysis in **pandas** before applying **scikit-learn**, **statsmodels**, or deep learning libraries.

    The basic library for plotting and visualizations in Python is **matplotlib**. It can be used to create static, animated, and interactive visualizations. **Seaborn** is a Python data visualization library based on **matplotlib**. It provides a high-level interface for drawing attractive and informative statistical graphics.

    In summary, the Python code for the practice chapters of the book utilize **scikit-learn, statsmodels, pandas, numpy, matplotlib**, and **seaborn**.

Import Python libraries

For the simple linear regression case study, we use **pandas** and **statsmodels**. First, we load the **pandas** library and the *ols* function from the **statsmodels** library. The abbreviation "ols" stands for ordinary least squares. Ordinary least squares is an alternative term for minimizing the sum of the squares of the residuals.

```python
import pandas as pd
from statsmodels.formula.api import ols
```

https://doi.org/10.1515/9781501505737-004

Load and verify data

We load the 'edincome.csv' file into a pandas dataframe *df*. A dataframe is the fundamental data structure in data science. It's a two-dimensional data structure consisting of rows and columns. In **pandas,** the rows and columns can also have associated labels.

We verify the first few records by using *.head()* method for dataframe objects. The result is shown in Figure 4.1.

```
df = pd.read_csv('data/edincome.csv')
df.head()
```

	Education	Income
0	10.0	32.1
1	10.4	36.5
2	10.7	23.9
3	11.1	52.3
4	11.4	30.2

Figure 4.1: First few records of edincome.csv dataset.

Run Regression – statsmodels

We run a simple linear regression using the *ols* function in the **statsmodels** library. The target variable is set as *Income* in units of $1,000K. The feature variable is set as *Education* in units of years. The results of the regression are stored in the object *slr*.

```
slr = ols('Income ~ Education',df).fit()
```

Review results and model performance

A summary report of the regression is displayed in Figure 4.2. The intercept is –23.2 and the coefficient corresponding to *Education* is 5.58. R-squared for the model is 0.878. Both the intercept and coefficient are statistically significant.

```
slr.summary()
```

OLS Regression Results

Dep. Variable:	Income	R-squared:	0.878
Model:	OLS	Adj. R-squared:	0.875
Method:	Least Squares	F-statistic:	238.4
Date:	Wed, 07 Jul 2021	Prob (F-statistic):	1.17e-16
Time:	21:10:07	Log-Likelihood:	-119.61
No. Observations:	35	AIC:	243.2
Df Residuals:	33	BIC:	246.3
Df Model:	1		
Covariance Type:	nonrobust		

	coef	std err	t	P>|t|	[0.025	0.975]
Intercept	-23.1764	5.918	-3.917	0.000	-35.216	-11.137
Education	5.5742	0.361	15.440	0.000	4.840	6.309

Omnibus:	2.854	Durbin-Watson:	2.535
Prob(Omnibus):	0.240	Jarque-Bera (JB):	1.726
Skew:	0.502	Prob(JB):	0.422
Kurtosis:	3.420	Cond. No.	75.8

Figure 4.2: Summary of the regression shows that both slope and intercept are statistically significant. The coefficients are shown in the **coef** column. R-squared is 0.878.

Make predictions

The *slr* object has a method *slr.predict( )*, which can be used to generate predictions for new data. We create a new dataframe *df_predict* with *Education* set at 12, 16, and 18. The dataframe is then used as the input to the *slr.predict( )* method. The results of the prediction are displayed in Figure 4.3. The model predicts that with 12 years of education, one can expect an income of $43.7K; with 16 years of education, an income of $66.0K; and with 18 years of education, an income of $77.2K.

```
data = {'Education': [12,16,18]}
df_predict = pd.DataFrame(data)
df_predict['Income'] = slr.predict(df_predict)
df_predict
```

	Education	Income
0	12	43.7
1	16	66.0
2	18	77.2

Figure 4.3: Predictions for new data.

5 K-Nearest Neighbors (KNN) – Concept

In this chapter, we introduce *classification* as the other principal form of supervised learning. In regression, we saw that the target variable is continuous. In classification, by contrast, the target variable is discrete. The simplest form of classification is *binary classification*, where the target variable has only two possible outcomes. In this chapter, we investigate binary classification using the K-Nearest Neighbors (KNN) algorithm. KNN is simple to understand and easy to implement. At the same time, it's a stepping stone to more sophisticated classification algorithms and approaches in machine learning.

> **Key Idea 1.** In classification, the target variable is *discrete*.
>
> **Key Idea 2.** In *binary classification*, the target variable has only two possible values.
>
> **Key Idea 3.** KNN can be used for regression or classification. When used for classifying a point p, KNN checks the classification of k (where k is an integer) of point p's nearest neighbors. It then assigns the majority value to the point.
>
> **Key Idea 4.** KNN relies on a *distance metric* to determine a point's nearest neighbors. The most commonly used distance metric in KNN is Euclidean distance.

5.1 Bird's Eye View

KNN is a machine learning algorithm for classification. What are some examples of classification? Using machine learning, we might attempt to classify email as spam or not-spam; determine whether a credit card transaction is fraudulent or not; evaluate whether a bank will grant a loan or not. These are all examples of *binary classification*, where we try to predict whether or not something belongs in some category.

If in the Olympic games we try to predict whether a participant will win gold, silver, bronze, or not medal, then the number of classes or categories is four. In classification, the number of categories can be small or quite large. In facial recognition, for example, where a picture is associated with a name, the number of possible names can be in the millions.

K-Nearest neighbors (KNN) starts from a simple intuition. If we want to know what an individual is like, check what its nearest neighbors are like. This seemingly ordinary intuition contains a subtle leap in thought. We have before us two things. We can ask, of course, whether the two things are *identical*. But we can also ask whether they are *similar*. If similar, what is their *degree of similarity*? With KNN, we are introduced to the idea of similarity as an abstract concept in machine learning.

Let's turn to KNN with an example. Suppose we want to predict how some person (p) will vote in an upcoming election. Will the person vote as a "Tory" or as a "Whig"? We will assume that there are only two choices.

https://doi.org/10.1515/9781501505737-005

As in all cases of machine learning, our attempt at prediction begins with data. We suppose that our dataset contains a record of early votes in the election. Can we apply KNN to predict how a person (p) will vote in the election using the record of early votes?

Under KNN, we check how k (where k is some integer) of person's neighbors voted. Imagine knocking on the door of five (k = 5) of p's closest neighbors and asking them how they voted. We then predict or "classify" person (p) as likely to vote Tory or Whig based on how the majority of the k neighbors voted.

In KNN, we always have to choose a value for k, where k is the number of neighbors to check. For example, if we set k = 1, we check only one nearest neighbor and see how they voted. If the nearest neighbor voted "Whig," we classify (p) as likely to vote "Whig." If the nearest neighbor voted "Tory," we classify (p) as likely to vote "Tory." If k = 3, then we check the votes of three of (p's) closest neighbors. We then take the majority of the three votes to decide (p's) classification. k is always odd to break any ties.

5.2 Prediction Structure

In Simple Linear Regression (SLR) we used a single feature variable x to predict a single target variable y. In SLR, both x and y are continuous.

$$\mathbf{x} \xrightarrow{predict} \mathbf{y}$$

In a later chapter, we will turn to multiple regression where multiple feature variables are used to predict a single continuous outcome y. In the case of multiple regression, the feature variables can be continuous or discrete.

$$\{x_1, x_2, \ldots, x_n\} \xrightarrow{predict} \mathbf{y}$$

Rather than writing out the feature variables as a list, we will represent multiple feature variables with a capital X.

$$\mathbf{X} \xrightarrow{predict} \mathbf{y}$$

What distinguishes regression from classification? In regression, the target variable is *always continuous*. By contrast, in classification the target variable is *always discrete*.

In summary, the KNN algorithm for classifying a new point p consists of three basic steps:

1. Choose an odd number k.
2. Check the classification of the k points nearest to p.
3. Assign the majority classification to point p.

Applying the KNN algorithm requires that we specify beforehand k, the number of neighbors we intend to check. We also need to know our *distance metric*, or how we intend to measure similarity. We examine distance metrics formally in the next chapter.

Montagues and Capulets in Verona

Let's look at KNN now with a simple example. Suppose we live in a town called Verona. Among the town's inhabitants are two rivalrous families: the Montagues and the Capulets. The families live in opposite sides of town since any contact between them breaks out in fights. As the town's managers, our goal is to minimize civil strife by keeping the two families separated as much as possible.

To continue our story, a stranger appears in town. We are informed that the stranger is a Montague or a Capulet, but we don't know which. Using KNN we need to classify the stranger as either a Montague or a Capulet, and then direct them to the right end of town.

To keep the example simple, we will use a *single feature* to predict the stranger's classification. Our dataset for prediction is a record of the eye color of all known Montagues and Capulets. In our toy example, eye color is measured on a simple scale from 1 to 10, ranging from light brown to jet black. Using eye color as our single feature variable, we will try to predict a *binary outcome*, i. e., whether the stranger is a Montague or a Capulet.

Table 5.1: List of eye color numbers for Capulets and Montagues.

color	family
.13	Capulet
.22	Capulet
.42	Capulet
3.23	Montague
6.22	Capulet
6.88	Montague
8.55	Montague

Table 5.1 displays a sample of the dataset. We see that the Capulets tend to have mostly brown eyes (lower values) and the Montagues mostly black eyes (higher values), though there are some exceptions. For example, among the exceptions is a Capulet with an eye color of 6.22. We also observe that the demarcation in eye color between Capulets and Montagues seems to be near the value 5. Those below 5 are mostly Capulets and those above are mostly Montagues.

Figure 5.1 shows the distribution of eye color for the two families. Capulets mostly have low values for eye color and Montagues mostly have high values. There is some overlap in the middle.

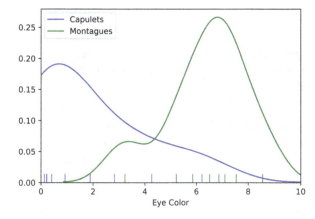

Figure 5.1: Eye color distribution for Capulets and Montagues. Capulets have lower eye color numbers. Montagues have higher eye color numbers.

Classifying a stranger

Let's apply the KNN algorithm now to predict whether Stranger One is a Montague or a Capulet.

1. We choose $k = 1$, the simplest setting for the algorithm. This means that we will check the classification of the closest neighbor.
2. We measure the stranger's eye color and it turns out to be 7.41. The closest point (eyecolor) in the dataset is 7.54, who happens to be a Montague. (Figure 5.2 shows the eye color value of Stranger One and the value and classification of the single nearest neighbor.)
3. Because the stranger's nearest neighbor is a Montague, we classify (predict) that the stranger is also a Montague.

Stranger One
(7.41)

Montague
(7.54)

Figure 5.2: Stranger One has an eye color of 7.41. He is closest to a Montague with an eye color of 7.54. Since $k = 1$, we classify Stranger One as a Montague.

Let's consider another stranger (Stranger Two) who appears in town. Stranger Two's eye color is 6.35. The nearest neighbor is 6.22, who is classified as a Capulet. Therefore, we classify Stranger Two as a Capulet. See Figure 5.3. In the case of Stranger Two, we probably have a mistaken classification. Why? Most Capulets tend to have brown eyes (range: 1–5) while most Montagues have black eyes (range: 6–10). Stranger Two is closest to the one of the few Capulets with darker black eyes, a value of 6.22.

Capulet
(6.22)

Stranger Two
(6.35)

Figure 5.3: Stranger Two has an eye color of 6.35. She is closest to a Capulet with an eye color of 6.22. Since k = 1, we classify Stranger Two as a Capulet.

Our toy example reveals that, in general, checking only one neighbor (k = 1) is not likely to be a good strategy. We might end up being close to an outlier. Or, if there is considerable noise in the data, our classifications can end up being highly inaccurate. What do we mean by noise in the data? One type of noise is measurement error. It's possible that the Capulet with an eye color of 6.22 is based on a mistaken recording. The individual's eye color might have been .622, but it was incorrectly recorded as 6.22.

Montague
(5.86)

Capulet
(6.22)

Stranger Two
(6.35)

Montague
(6.52)

Figure 5.4: If k = 3, Stranger Two's nearest neighbors are Montague (5.86), Capulet (6.22), and Montague (6.52). Stranger Two is, therefore, classified as a Montague.

What happens if we increase the value of k from k = 1 to k = 3? The three nearest neighbors now are: Montague, Capulet, and Montague. See Figure 5.4. The majority classification of Stranger Two's three nearest neighbors turns out, therefore, to be a Montague.

In summary, our toy example illustrates how the town of Verona might use machine learning to classify an arbitrary stranger as either a Montague or a Capulet.

5.3 Case Study: To Loan or Not to Loan

Now that we have an intuitive idea of how classification works with KNN, let's consider a more realistic scenario. Our case study involves the Verona Savings and Loan (VSL) bank. VSL is expanding to other cities. As a way of scaling up its loan processing volume, VSL is considering using machine learning to supplement the work of human loan processors.

Dataset

As with all machine learning models, VSL's starting point is historical data. Table 5.2 shows sample rows, each row corresponding to a loan application. The first column records an individual's yearly *Income* in dollars. The second column records their *Credit Score* ranging from 0 to 800. The final column *Status* records whether the individual received the loan (1) or was denied (0).

Table 5.2: The loan approval table includes *Income*, *Credit Score*, and *Status* as variables.

Income	Credit Score	Status
74637	511	0
132564	610	1
106113	588	1
85149	556	0
100279	575	1

Figure 5.5 is a scatterplot of the data. The *x*-axis represents yearly income, the *y*-axis represents credit score, and the color whether the loan was granted (grey) or denied (black).

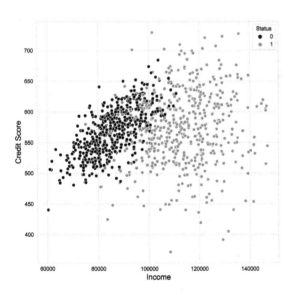

Figure 5.5: A scatterplot of loan approvals with *Income* on the *x*-axis and *Credit Score* on the *y*-axis. A "1" (grey) means that the loan was approved. A "0" (black) means that the loan was denied.

Table 5.3 provides summary statistics of the loan approvals dataset, including mean, standard deviation, maximum, and minimum.

Table 5.3: Summary Statistics for Loans.

Statistic	Income	Credit Score	Status
count	1000	1000	1000
mean	99,813.5	570.2	0.5
std	18,150.8	50.5	.5
min	60,322.0	372.0	0/0
50 %	97,740.0	571.0	0.5
max	146,875.0	729.0	1.0

Applying KNN

We are now ready to apply KNN to loan processing. Figure 5.6 shows a scatterplot of the historical dataset and four *unclassified* points. The unclassified points (appearing as stars) are new loan applications. The KNN machine learning model needs to determine whether to grant or deny the loan based on the point's similarity to neighboring points.

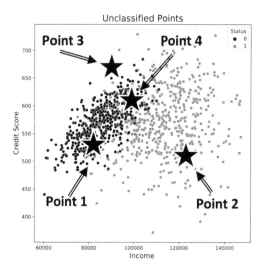

Figure 5.6: Given a KNN model, we want to classify the four new points represented as stars.

From a visual inspection of Figure 5.6, we might project that Point 1 will be rejected since most of its neighboring points are rejections. Similarly, Point 2 is likely to be accepted since most of the neighboring points are approved loans. It's unclear, however, how KNN might classify Points 3 and 4. Both seem to fall near rejected clusters, but there are enough neighboring accepted points to sway the classification.

KNN Classification

If we run KNN classification on the dataset, we get the following results. We give detailed explanations of how to evaluate classification models in Chapter 10. Overall accuracy of the model for $k = 3$ is: 0.93.

The confusion matrix for the KNN classification is shown in Figure 5.7. Starting from the top left quadrant and going clockwise, the confusion matrix shows True Negatives (TN), False Negatives (FN), True Positives (TP), and False Positives (FP).

Predicted

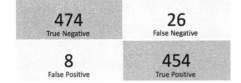

Actual

474 True Negative	**26** False Negative
8 False Positive	**454** True Positive

Figure 5.7: The KNN confusion matrix for $k = 3$. The top left box represents True Negatives (94.8%). The bottom right box represents True Positives (90.8%).

The classification report for the KNN classification is shown in Figure 5.8.

```
              precision    recall  f1-score   support

           0       0.91      0.95      0.93       500
           1       0.95      0.91      0.93       500

    accuracy                           0.93      1000
   macro avg       0.93      0.93      0.93      1000
weighted avg       0.93      0.93      0.93      1000
```

Figure 5.8: The KNN classification report for $k = 3$. F1-score is the harmonic mean of the precision and recall scores. For the case study, the F1-score is 0.93 for both loan approval and loan denied.

Predictions

If we run KNN against the historical dataset, Figure 5.9 shows how the four points are classified by the KNN classifier differently, depending on choices for $k = 3$ vs. $k = 5$. The left panel shows the four unclassified points as stars. The middle panel shows the results for $k = 3$ and the right panel shows the results for $k = 5$. Rejected loans are shown with a cross and accepted loans are shown as diamonds.

As expected, Points 1 and 2 are classified as 0 (denied) and 1 (granted) when $k = 3$ or $k = 5$. Point 3 is classified as 0 (denied) for both $k = 3$ and $k = 5$. Point 4 is classified as 1 (granted) under $k = 3$, but 0 (denied) under $k = 5$. The results are summarized in Table 5.4.

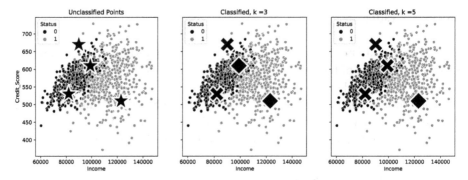

Figure 5.9: The left panel displays four unclassified points. The middle panel displays their classification with $k = 3$. The right panel displays their classification with $k = 5$.

Table 5.4: Classification of new loans by $k = 3$ and $k = 5$.

Point	$k = 3$	$k = 5$
Point 1	Denied	Denied
Point 2	Granted	Granted
Point 3	Denied	Denied
Point 4	Granted	Denied

5.4 Summary

In this chapter, we introduced classification as a major form of supervised learning alongside regression. In classification, the aim of prediction is to classify an item as belonging to a class or a category. Binary classification is a special case where the category has only two possible values. We then used the KNN algorithm for classification. KNN is based on a simple idea: in order to classify an item, check the properties of the item's nearest neighbors. We also saw that KNN relies on a distance metric to determine the nearness of points.

6 K-Nearest Neighbors (KNN) – Theory

In the previous, we began our study of classification with the KNN algorithm. We saw that KNN's rests on a simple intuition: if we want to classify a point, check what its neighbors are like. Our first goal in this chapter is to make precise the idea of *likeness* or *similarity* by surveying some common distance metrics as used in machine learning. Our second goal is to present a technique for choosing a value for k in the KNN algorithm. In the last chapter, we guessed some values for k. In this chapter, we take a systematic approach for choosing values for k. Finally, we use the technique as a springboard to discuss the advantages of creating a *pipeline* to automate parts of the machine learning workflow.

> **Key Idea 1.** KNN employs a *distance metric* to determine the nearest neighbors of a point.
>
> **Key Idea 2.** There is a *variety* of distance metrics in machine learning. The most common is Euclidean distance, but there are other metrics such as cosine distance.
>
> **Key Idea 3.** In KNN, k is a *hyperparameter*. Machine learning models learn the values of *parameters* during training. By contrast, hyperparameter values are set before training begins, as part of model tuning.
>
> **Key Idea 4.** In KNN we can choose a value for k by testing a range of values and seeing which produces the lowest Mean Squared Error (MSE).
>
> **Key Idea 5.** A machine learning *workflow* is the series of steps involved in model development. A machine learning *pipeline* automates elements of the ML workflow.

6.1 Distance Metrics

In this section we survey several distance metrics. In machine learning a distance metric is a *formal method* for measuring the distance or closeness between two points. Closeness is synonymous with similarity.

Euclidean distance

The most common distance metric is Euclidean distance. It captures our ordinary understanding of distance. In one dimension (Figure 6.1), the distance d between two points **a** and **b** is the absolute value of the difference in their x coordinates:

$$d(\mathbf{a}, \mathbf{b}) = |x_a - x_b|$$

https://doi.org/10.1515/9781501505737-006

Figure 6.1: Euclidean distance in one dimension.

A rise in temperature from −10 Celsius to 18 Celsius, for example, is calculated as the absolute value of the difference in the two temperatures: $|{-10} - 18| = 28$.

In two dimensions (Figure 6.2), the distance can be calculated using the Pythagorean theorem:

$$d(\mathbf{a}, \mathbf{b}) = \sqrt{(x_a - x_b)^2 + (y_a - y_b)^2}$$

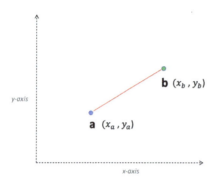

Figure 6.2: Euclidean distance in two dimensions.

In three dimensions (Figure 6.3), we add another term z, representing the third dimension, to calculate the distance:

$$d(\mathbf{a}, \mathbf{b}) = \sqrt{(x_a - x_b)^2 + (y_a - y_b)^2 + (z_a - z_b)^2}$$

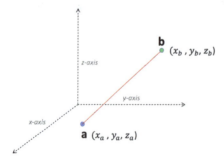

Figure 6.3: Euclidean distance in three dimensions.

As we progress with our study, we will see that machine learning is all about higher dimensions. Fortunately, Euclidean distance generalizes easily to n-dimensions.

In order to express Euclidean distance in higher dimensions we will use the more compact notation of vectors. The Euclidean distance between two vectors **x** and **y** in *n-dimensions* can be expressed as:

$$d(\mathbf{x}, \mathbf{y}) = \sqrt{\sum_{i=1}^{n}(x_n - y_n)^2} \qquad (6.1)$$

where **x** and **y** are vectors and n is the number of dimensions:

$$\mathbf{x} = (x_1, x_2, \ldots, x_n) \quad \text{and} \quad \mathbf{y} = (y_1, y_2, \ldots, y_n)$$

Manhattan distance

Euclidean distance is a perfectly good distance metric in many circumstances. Unfortunately, it doesn't always work. It doesn't work, for example, for measuring distances when we are driving in New York city. Let's see why.

If we hail a taxicab in Manhattan, the shortest distance of traversal is *not* Euclidean distance. The path of travel in taxicabs is constrained by the geometry of the roads, which are laid out in grids.

Suppose we go from Grand Central Station (Point **a**) to the Museum of Modern Art (Point **b**), as shown in Figure 6.4. The distance traversed by the taxicab is the sum of the horizontal and vertical distances, not the straight path from **a** to **b**. This is called Manhattan distance or taxicab distance.

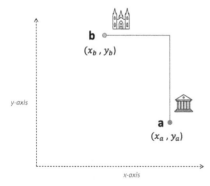

Figure 6.4: Manhattan Distance in two dimensions is calculated by adding the vertical and horizontal distances.

Manhattan distance is calculated by adding the vertical and horizontal distances.

$$d(\mathbf{a}, \mathbf{b}) = |x_b - x_a| + |y_b - y_a|$$

In n-dimensions, Manhattan distance between two vectors can be expressed as:

$$d(\mathbf{x}, \mathbf{y}) = \sum_{i=1}^{n} |x_n - y_n| \tag{6.2}$$

Once again, x and y are vectors and n is the number of dimensions:

$$\mathbf{x} = (x_1, x_2, \ldots, x_n) \quad \text{and} \quad \mathbf{y} = (y_1, y_2, \ldots, y_n)$$

Minkowski distance

Euclidean and Manhattan distances are special cases of Minkowski distance. The general formula for Minkowski Distance is:

$$d(\mathbf{x}, \mathbf{y}) = \left(\sum_{i=1}^{n} |x_n - y_n|^p \right)^{\frac{1}{p}} \tag{6.3}$$

The formula seems daunting. We should observe that for $p = 1$, Minkowski distance collapses readily to Manhattan distance. For $p = 2$, the formula collapses to Euclidean distance.

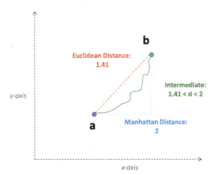

Figure 6.5: Minkowski Distance can be used to calculated intermediate distances.

Why do we need the more general notion of Minkowski distance? In some cases an intermediate value for p (e. g. 1.5) between Euclidean and Manhattan distance might be appropriate. Imagine walking on a trail that meanders from point **a** to point **b**. The length of the journey is intermediate between Manhattan and Euclidean distance, as shown in Figure 6.5.

Hamming Distance

Another useful distance metric is the Hamming Distance. It is one of the simplest methods for comparing the similarity of two strings. The Hamming distance between two strings of equal length is the number of positions in which they differ.

wonderful	wondarful	1
wonderful	wanderfll	2
wonderful	wunderbar	3

Figure 6.6: Hamming Distance compares disagreements in two strings.

For example, Figure 6.6 shows the Hamming distance between pairs of strings. Hamming distance is often stated in *standardized* form, meaning we divide the number of disagreements in a vector by the length of the vector. This provides the Hamming distance as a number between 0 and 1.

Hamming distance is often handy when comparing two binary arrays of equal length. There are cases in machine learning, for example, where all the features are composed of dummy 'Boolean' features. In such a case, the Hamming distance is useful for calculating the distance between two observations.

Cosine distance

The idea of cosine similarity or cosine distance originates from the world of trigonometry. The intuition behind cosine distance and cosine similarity is that we are interested in the *angle* between two vectors, not the ordinary distance between them.

Let's consider an example to motivate our understanding of cosine distance and how it works compared to Euclidean distance. Suppose we have three music listeners (A, B, C) and ten songs. We represent the music listening pattern for each listener as an array:

Listener A: [8 9 8 0 0 0 0 0 0 7]

Listener B: [4 3 2 3 0 0 1 0 0 3]

Listener C: [0 0 0 1 0 4 3 2 3 0]

Listener A has listened to the first song 8 times, the second song 9 times, and so on. Listener B listens to mostly the same songs as Listener A, although not as frequently. Listener C listens to mostly all different songs from Listeners A and B. If we calculate Euclidean distances, it turns out that Listener B is "closer" to Listener C than to Listener A, even though Listener B and A listen to the same songs. Cosine distances, however, gives the result we expect. Listener B is "closer" to Listener A than Listener C in terms of cosine distance. The distance measurements are shown in Table 6.1.

Table 6.1: Euclidean vs. Cosine Distance.

Listener Pair	Euclidean Distance	Cosine Distance
A, B	10.68	.14
B, C	8.66	.86

It's impossible to visualize vectors in higher dimensions, but we can imagine flattening out the vectors representing listeners A, B, and C as shown in Figure 6.7.

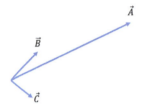

Figure 6.7: Three Vectors A, B, and C.

Figure 6.8 shows Euclidean distances between vectors A,B and vectors B,C. The Euclidean distance from A,B (the distance from the tip of A to the tip of B) is greater than the distance from B,C. Using Euclidean distance as a metric, B is further away from A than from C.

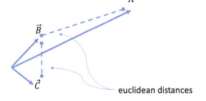

euclidean distances

Figure 6.8: The Euclidean distance between two vectors is the distance between the tips of the two vectors.

Figure 6.9 shows, however, that the angular distance between A,B is smaller than that between B,C. Using cosine distance as a metric, B is closer to A than to C.

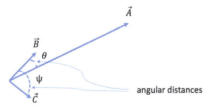

angular distances

Figure 6.9: The angular distance between two vectors is the angle between them.

Calculating cosine distance or similarity

Recall from trigonometry that the cosine of the angle θ between two non-zero vectors is:

$$cos(\theta) = \frac{A \cdot B}{\|A\|\|B\|}$$

Cosine similarity is just that:

$$cos(\theta) = \frac{A \cdot B}{\|A\|\|B\|} \qquad (6.4)$$

Cosine similarity is a way of measuring the "angular distance" or "angular separation" between two vectors.

Recommendation systems based on "collaborative filtering" employ cosine similarity. We build a vector for each user and then calculate their similarity using cosine similarity. In comparing two listeners, we want to match on which of the same songs they listened to, *not* which songs they didn't listen to. In a music catalog with millions of songs, what counts are the items the two listeners listened to. This highlights a crucial difference between calculations for cosine distance and Hamming distance. The latter also matches on what two listeners didn't listen to.

The cosine distance technique also works for comparing document similarity. Instead of the number of listens or views, each row is a document and each column represents the number of times a particular word appears in the text. This approach is called "bag of words" since we are not looking at the order of words, but just comparing the frequency of words in a text.

Figure 6.10 shows the frequency of word appearances in four texts: *Othello*, *Hamlet*, *Moby Dick*, and *Piazza Tales*. The table shows columns for only a few words. The full table contains a column for every word appearance in the four texts. *Othello* and *Hamlet* were authored by Shakespeare. *Moby Dick* and *Piazza Tales* were authored by Melville.

	crucifix	crucifixion	cruel	cruell	cruellest	crueltie	cruelty	cruet	cruise	cruised
othello	0	0	0	3	0	1	0	0	0	0
hamlet	0	0	2	0	0	0	0	0	0	0
mobydick	1	1	8	0	2	0	1	4	9	1
piazzatales	3	0	2	0	0	0	2	0	2	2

Figure 6.10: A table showing 'bag of words' for four texts. The rows are the texts. Columns are specific words. The value is the occurrence of that word in the text.

	othello	hamlet	mobydick	piazzatales
othello	1.00	0.33	0.22	0.18
hamlet	0.33	1.00	0.32	0.28
mobydick	0.22	0.32	1.00	0.64
piazzatales	0.18	0.28	0.64	1.00

Figure 6.11: A table showing cosine similarity of four texts by Shakespeare and Melville. As expected, Hamlet and Othello (both by Shakespeare) are closer to each other than to Moby Dick and Piazza Tales (both by Melville). Similarly, Moby Dick and Piazza Tales are closer to each other than to Othello or Hamlet.

When we run a cosine similarity for the four texts, the results are shown in Figure 6.11. The entire comparison can be run with a few lines of code using natural language processing libraries such as NLTK, which stands for Natural Language Toolkit.

As expected, the closest text to *Moby Dick* is *Piazza Tales*. Both were written by Melville. The closest text to *Othello* is *Hamlet*. Both were written by Shakespeare.

6.2 Choosing *k* in KNN

We saw in the previous chapter that the KNN algorithm requires choosing a value for *k*. In machine learning, a *hyperparameter* is a variable whose value is set before the learning process begins. By contrast, the values for *parameters* are learned during training. In this section, we provide a technique for choosing *k*. We caution though that the technique is meant to be suggestive, not definitive. The actual choice of *k* in a production model will be influenced by a range of factors.

The basic technique is to try a *range of values* for *k* and see which one produces the smallest error. In a previous chapter, we introduced Mean Squared Error (MSE) as a standard metric to evaluate the discrepancy or error between the actual value and the predicted value from the model.

For a single observation, the error is:

$$\epsilon = y - \hat{y}$$

As a review, the MSE for a model is the Residual Sum of Squares divided by the number of observations n:

$$\widehat{MSE} = \frac{RSS}{n}$$

where,

$$RSS = \sum_{i=1}^{n}(y_i - \hat{y}_i)^2$$

The pseudo-code for calculating MSE is as follows:

- Create an empty list called 'errors' to store MSE for each k.
- Create a loop which iterates over a range of k (e. g., k = 1 to 15)
  - Calculate MSE for current k.
  - Add the MSE value to the "errors" list. The list is indexed by k.
  - Increment k by 1.
- Retrieve the value of k where MSE begins to plateau.
- Plot MSE values against k.

Let's apply the technique now to our Loan Case Study from the previous chapter. Table 6.2 shows sample data of k vs MSE. Figure 6.12 is a plot of Mean Squared Error with increasing k.

Table 6.2: A table showing Mean Squared Error for different choices of k.

k	MSE
1	0.139
2	0.139
3	0.123
4	0.129
5	0.117

Figure 6.12: Mean Squared Error (MSE) drops as k increases. However, MSE plateaus near k = 10.

We can see from the plot that the Mean Squared Error declines sharply as we increase the value from k = 1 to k = 11. Afterwards, the error plateaus. From the analysis, we can conclude that setting k = 11, or thereabouts, is a good choice based on the data.

6.3 ML Pipelines, Hyperparameters

In choosing a value for k, we have also created a very basic machine learning pipeline. An ML pipeline automates the workflow for creating ML models. Figure 6.13 shows the machine learning workflow from an enterprise perspective.

Machine Learning Workflow

Ingestion   Cleaning   Preprocessing   Modeling   Deployment

Figure 6.13: Model development life cycle from an enterprise information technology perspective.

Each step in the ML workflow requires careful thought and a detailed architecture. At the beginning of the pipeline is data ingestion. Most enterprises have data stored in variety of databases. The data exists in both structured and unstructured form and in various states of readiness. A core element of building a pipeline at the ingestion layer is to automate drawing in data from disparate sources. Data cleaning and pre-processing includes converting the data into an input format that can be processed by the model algorithm. Character data, for example, has to converted to numeric data. Next is modeling. During this step, we train a model by accepting inputs to predict an output. This step includes model tuning, including choosing values for the hyper-parameters. We saw an elementary example of how to test various values for k using MSE. But more realistic examples means automatically testing various combinations of multiple hyperparameters. Model validation might also involve running field pilots before a model is deployed to production.

6.4 Summary

In this chapter, we began by looking at a variety of distance metrics, beginning with the familiar Euclidean distance. We then briefly looked at other distance metrics, including Manhattan distance, Minkowski distance, and cosine distance. Next, we provided a heuristic for choosing a value for k in KNN models. We noted that k is a hyper-parameter, which is chosen by humans. By contrast, parameter values are discovered by the machine algorithm. Finally, we outlined some of the steps involved in a machine learning workflow.

7 K-Nearest Neighbors (KNN) – Practice

The KNN case study involves Verona Savings and Loan (VSL) bank. VSL's goal is to implement a machine learning model, based on KNN, to predict loan grants.

Import Python libraries

We load **pandas** and **numpy** libraries. We use **scikit-learn** for the KNN classifier. We load the classifier along with functions to generate confusion matrix, classifier report, and accuracy score.

```
import pandas as pd
import numpy as np

from sklearn.neighbors import KNeighborsClassifier
from sklearn.metrics import confusion_matrix,
        classification_report, accuracy_score
```

Load and verify data

We load the dataset into the *df* dataframe. The first few records are shown in Figure 7.1. For the model, we use *Income* and *Credit_Score* as the feature variables and *Status* as the target variable. A *Status* of 1 means that the loan was granted, and a *Status* of 0 means that the loan was denied.

```
df = pd.read_csv("data/loans.csv").round(1)
df.head()
```

	Income	Credit_Score	Status
0	86499.0	575.7	0
1	106113.7	588.0	1
2	100279.1	575.9	0
3	113616.9	559.0	1
4	135667.3	727.1	1

Figure 7.1: First few records of loan dataset.

https://doi.org/10.1515/9781501505737-007

Run KNN classifier

The first two lines create X and y as the feature and target variables. The next two lines create and fit the two classifiers. The first classifier uses $k = 3$. The second uses $k = 5$.

```
X = df.drop(['Status'],axis=1)
y = df['Status']

knn3 = KNeighborsClassifier(n_neighbors=3).fit(X,y)
knn5 = KNeighborsClassifier(n_neighbors=5).fit(X,y)
```

Evaluate classifier

We show evaluations of the $k = 3$ classifier using accuracy score, confusion matrix, and classification report.

Accuracy Score

The accuracy score for the classifier with $k = 3$ is excellent at 0.93.

```
y_pred = knn3.predict
print(accuracy_score(y,y_pred))
```

Accuracy Score: 0.93

Confusion Matrix

The confusion matrix for $k = 3$ is shown in Figure 7.2.

```
print(confusion_matrix(y,y_pred))
```

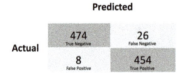

Figure 7.2: Confusion Matrix, $k = 3$.

Classification Report

The classification report for $k = 3$ is shown in Figure 7.3. The model does well with both precision and recall. The combined f1-score is .93.

```
print(classification_report(y,y_pred))
```

```
              precision    recall  f1-score   support

           0       0.91      0.95      0.93       500
           1       0.95      0.91      0.93       500

    accuracy                           0.93      1000
   macro avg       0.93      0.93      0.93      1000
weighted avg       0.93      0.93      0.93      1000
```

Figure 7.3: Classification Report, $k = 3$.

Make predictions

Using classifiers for $k = 3$ and $k = 5$, we generate predictions for four new points with the structure [Income, Credit Score]. The predictions are the same for Points 1, 2, 3 but different for Point 4. The results are shown in Figure 7.4.

```
new_points =[[82000,530],[123000,510],[90000,670],[99000,610]]
y_pred_3 = knn3.predict(new_points)
y_pred_5 = knn5.predict(new_points)


data = {'KNN=3': y_pred_3, 'KNN=5': y_pred_5}
pd.DataFrame.from_dict(data, orient='index',
    columns=['Point1','Point2','Point3','Point4'])
```

	Point1	Point2	Point3	Point4
KNN=3	0	1	0	1
KNN=5	0	1	0	0

Figure 7.4: Predictions for Four New Points with Classifiers $k = 3$ and $k = 5$.

Part II: **Model Assessment**

8 Model Assessment – Bias-Variance Tradeoff

This is the first of three chapters on assessing model accuracy. In this chapter, we delineate model development as a form of *optimization*: the best models strike a balance between *minimizing error* and *maximizing generalization*. In the next chapter, we focus on metrics for assessing regression models. In the final chapter, we do the same for classification models.

> **Key Idea 1.** The true test for gauging model accuracy is to see how the model performs against new, *unseen* data. The ability to perform well against unseen data is referred to as *model generalization*.
>
> **Key Idea 2.** In order to evaluate model generalization, supervised machine learning datasets are split into two parts: a training set and a test set. The training set is used to train the model. The test set is used to evaluate the model.
>
> **Key Idea 3.** *K*-fold cross-validation takes the train-split idea one step further by *partitioning* the data into *k-folds*. Train and test is conducted *k-times* against various partitions and, at the end, an average evaluation score is returned.
>
> **Key Idea 4.** Model development is subject to two extreme imbalances: *underfitting* and *overfitting*. In underfitting, the model is unable to capture the underlying trend in the data. In overfitting, the model incorporates too much of the underlying noise.
>
> **Key Idea 5.** Model development is a tradeoff between minimizing error and maximizing generalization. Simpler models are poor at minimizing error (*high bias*) but better at maximizing generalization (*low variance*). Complex models are better at minimizing error (*low bias*) but poor at maximizing generalization (*high variance*). The best models achieve an optimum balance in the Bias-Variance Tradeoff.

8.1 Train-Test Split

In this chapter, we begin by examining two techniques which assist with the task of model optimization. The first technique, as shown in Figure 8.1, splits the data into two parts: a *training set* and a *test set*. The second technique, called *k-fold cross-validation*, takes the test-train split idea one step further. The dataset is randomly split into *k* partitions or *folds*. The model is then trained and tested multiple times (*k-times*), instead of once, to calculate average model accuracy. Model development during the test and train phase is subject to two major imbalances: *underfitting* and *overfitting*. We describe how this occurs. Finally, we discuss the *Bias-Variance Tradeoff*, which is the underling theoretical reason why there is an inherent tension between minimizing model error and maximizing model generalization.

A student studies for an exam by practicing. The practice is a set of questions. On the day of the exam, the exam questions turn out to be exactly the same as the practice questions. In such a scenario we are unlikely to say that a student has learned the material. We would be more likely to say that the student has memorized it. Learning

https://doi.org/10.1515/9781501505737-008

is not memorization. The same principle applies in machine learning. The true test of learning is being able to perform accurately when presented with new, unseen data.

Figure 8.1: The dataset is split into two portions, one for training and the other for testing.

In supervised learning, therefore, the true test for assessing model accuracy is to see how a model performs against new, unseen data. It is customary, therefore, to split the original dataset into two parts. A larger portion of the data is used for training the model. A smaller, unseen portion is held out for testing. If a model is able to make accurate predictions against the unseen, test dataset, we say that the model is able to generalize.

8.2 *K*-Fold Cross-Validation

We can take the train-test split one step further by using cross-validation. In cross-validation, the data is split not once but several times. The model is then trained and tested against different "folds" or partitions. The average score is then used as the overall score.

The most commonly used method of cross-validation is *K*-Fold cross-validation, where k is usually 5 or 10. When performing 5-fold cross-validation, for example, the data is split into five partitions ("folds") of equal size. The first model is trained against the first four folds and tested against the last fold. In the second iteration, the model is trained against another set of four folds and tested against the remaining fold. The process is repeated five times so that each fold appears as a test set. After collecting five accuracy values, we then compute the average accuracy. In *K*-Fold cross-validation, the model is trained and tested on multiple samples. The process is illustrated in Figure 8.2. The obvious advantage of cross-validation is that the model is evaluated against multiple random slices of the data.

8.3 Underfit and Overfit

Let's now look more closely at the training and test process. During the training process, the model is susceptible to flaws at two extremes: underfitting or overfitting. In the case of underfitting, the model has not learned enough to generalize. In the case of overfitting, the model has learned too much. Underfitting arises when the model is too simple or underpowered. Overfitting occurs when the model is too complex or overpowered. We can think of underfitting as an arrow falling short of the mark and

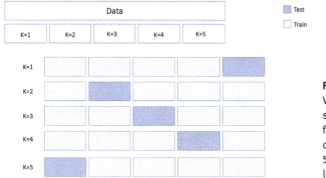

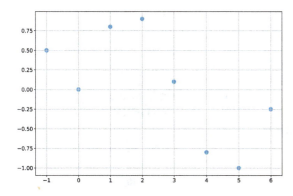

Figure 8.2: In *K*-Fold Cross-Validation, the dataset is split into *k* partitions or folds. In the figure, the original dataset is split into 5 folds. Each fold appears at least once in the test set.

overfitting as an arrow over shooting the mark. Simpler models are prone to underfitting, while complex models are prone to overfitting.

To motivate our understanding of underfitting and overfitting, let's consider a simple case where we have a small number of data points, as in Figure 8.3.

Figure 8.3: Scatterplot of a set of points.

We are already familiar with using simple linear regression as a model to fit the data. If we do so, the model is a straight line. A simple linear regression fit of the data points is shown in the top left panel in Figure 8.4. We also know how to quantify the error in the model using Mean Squared Error (MSE).

But we are not constrained to using a straight line as our model. We can try fitting the data with a slightly more complex model, a quadratic equation of the form:

$$y = \beta_0 + \beta_1 x + \beta_2 x^2$$

A polynomial fit of degree 2 for the data points is shown in the top right panel of Figure 8.4. As in the case of linear regression, the polynomial fit also returns an intercept and a set of coefficients. For the data points, the quadratic fit turns out to

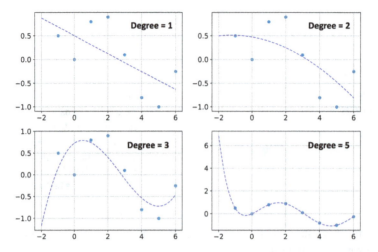

Figure 8.4: The top left panel is simple linear regression, with a polynomial of degree 1. The top right panel is a regression based on a polynomial of degree 2. The bottom left panel is a regression based on a polynomial of degree 3. The bottom right panel is a regression based on a polynomial of degree 4. Increasing the polynomial degree leads to better fits or smaller training errors.

have the equation:

$$y = -0.02 + -0.06x + 0.48x^2$$

If we quantify the errors using MSE, error for the quadratic model turns out to be less than that for simple linear regression. The polynomial of degree 2 is "closer" to the points than a polynomial of degree 1.

We can keep going using polynomials of higher degrees, as shown in the bottom panels of Figure 8.4. We can achieve better fits of the data using ever increasing higher-order polynomials. From the figures it's apparent that higher degrees of polynomials correspond to better fits and less error.

Figure 8.5 shows the corresponding reduction in errors. The thing to notice is that the errors decrease with greater "model complexity," where model complexity corresponds to higher-order polynomials.

The phenomenon of reducing model error by increasing model complexity applies not just to our simple dataset, but is a general rule in machine learning. Given any set of data points, it possible to find a model (or mathematical function) that approaches a perfect fit asymptotically. This phenomenon is shown in Figure 8.6.

The astute reader is surely thinking: Why not reduce model error during the training process by increasing model complexity? Can't we achieve near perfect accuracy by using ever more complex models? The answer is yes, but greater accuracy during the training phase comes with a cost during the test phase.

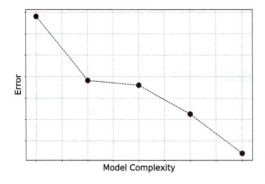

Model Complexity

Figure 8.5: As model complexity increases, error (mean squared error) decreases.

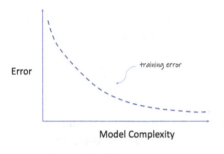

Model Complexity

Figure 8.6: Training error decreases as model complexity increases.

Let's look at Figure 8.7, which shows the pattern of error for the test set. As we increase model complexity, model error during the training phase decreases. But as we increase model complexity, test error decreases initially but an inflection point is reached when it begins to shoot upward.

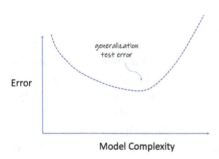

Model Complexity

Figure 8.7: Test error decreases at first with an increase in model complexity. But an inflection point is reached where error begins to increase.

Looking at the different pattern of error in train vs. test gives us a basis for precisely defining overfitting. Figure 8.8 displays two models, A and B. Model B has a lower training error than model A. However, model B's test error is higher.

Overfitting occurs when training error for some model (e. g., model B) is lower than another model (e. g., model A), but the test error for the model B is greater than that for model A. The comparison is shown in Figure 8.8.

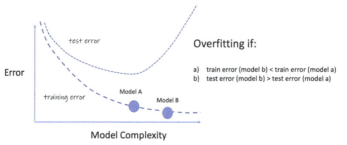

Overfitting if:

a) train error (model b) < train error (model a)
b) test error (model b) > test error (model a)

Figure 8.8: Model B has a lower training error than Model A, but it has a larger test error compared to Model A. This discrepancy is a sign of overfittting.

8.4 Bias-Variance Tradeoff

Why do we see different patterns of error during train and test? The reason is that there are different sources of error in the data: *noise*, *bias*, and *variance*.

Noise

The first source of error is noise. Noise is *ineliminable error* due to randomness. Randomness in data manifests itself in a variety of guises. Some noise is due to errors in measurement. Others are due to properties of one or more of the variables. It's just a fact we have to live with. It's a principal reason why the error term ϵ never goes down to 0.

Bias

The second source of error is bias. Bias is the difference between the average fit of a model and the true function. The "true" function produces the data, but we can never know it directly. We can think of the true function as the underlying law of nature or phenomenon we are trying to model. Let's assume for the moment that for a particular dataset the true function is a third-order polynomial. No matter how "hard" a straight line tries to approximate a third-order polynomial, there will always be a difference. A straight line has only two degrees of freedom. It can change its slope or its intercept. Given those two degrees of freedom there will always be a discrepancy (bias) between the true model and the linear model. By contrast, a second order polynomial has an additional degree of freedom compared to a first order polynomial. Thus, it has more flexibility (*lower bias*) in fitting the data points. In general, models with lower complexity have higher bias because they have less flexibility in fitting the data.

Variance

The third source of error is variance. Variance refers to the amount some function must change if presented with a new dataset. In the context of machine learning, variance comes up because we don't know the true function. We also have available limited samples of the data generated by the true function. Given a sample dataset, the machine learning algorithm estimates the function. When presented with different datasets, the algorithm comes up with different estimates for the true function. In the ideal case, the different estimates should not vary greatly. However, with some methods, small changes in the dataset lead to large changes in the estimate. It turns out that models with lesser flexibility (high bias) tend to have low variance across different training samples. At the same time, models with greater flexibility (low bias) tend to have high variance across different samples. As we increase model complexity, variance between fits can get quite large. In general, high-complexity models have low bias but high variance.

In short, there is a natural tradeoff between bias and variance. The goal of model development is to find a sweet spot where we have minimized the error, but not too much so as to sacrifice generalizability.

8.5 Summary

In this chapter, we formulated a related set of principles for evaluating model accuracy. Machine learning models must strike a balance between minimizing error and maximizing generalization. We can reduce error by increasing model complexity. But this single-minded approach comes with a severe penalty. The model is not able to deal as accurately with unseen data. At the other end of the scale, we can maximize generality, but it means working with simpler models prone to greater error due to bias. The optimal model, therefore, strikes a balance between bias and variance. In practical terms, this balance is achieved by splitting the data into train and test. A more rigorous approach to the split is to use techniques such as K-Fold cross-validation.

9 Model Assessment – Regression

In this chapter, we discuss two principal methods for assessing regression models: MSE and R^2. First, we briefly review Mean Squared Error (MSE), a concept which we defined in an earlier chapter. The bulk of this chapter examines in detail the concept of R^2 (pronounced "R squared").

Key Idea 1. A primary metric for evaluating model accuracy is Mean Squared Error (MSE). MSE is the average of squared errors, where error (ϵ) is defined as the difference between the observed value (y) and the predicted value ($\hat{y}$).

Key Idea 2. A second metric for evaluating regression model accuracy is R^2, also called the *coefficient of determination*. R^2 is a *ratio*: it compares performance of the regression model against a *baseline* model. R^2 is always a number between 0 and 1.

Key Idea 3. R^2 is also the proportion of the variance in the target variable that is said to be *explained* by the feature variables in the regression model.

9.1 Mean Squared Error

We saw in earlier chapters that the regression model minimizes the Residual Sum of Squares (RSS). RSS measures the error or discrepancy between observed data and predicted data. It was defined formally as:

$$\widehat{RSS} \equiv \sum_{i=1}^{n} \epsilon_i^2 = \sum_{i=1}^{n} (y_i - \hat{y}_i)^2$$

We also saw that Mean Squared Error (MSE) is just RSS divided by the number of observations (n):

$$\widehat{MSE} = \frac{RSS}{n}$$

MSE can be defined directly as:

$$\widehat{MSE} = \frac{1}{n} \sum_{i=1}^{n} (y_i - \hat{y}_i)^2$$

When comparing two models against the same data, we can conclude that the model with a lower MSE is more accurate or has less error. Because MSE depends on the choice of units, it can't be used to compare models which use different units for the data. This is where R^2 comes to the rescue.

https://doi.org/10.1515/9781501505737-009

9.2 R^2 – Intuition

Also called the coefficient of determination, R^2 explains the proportion of variation in the data that is accounted for by the model. The value of R^2 is dimensionless. R^2 compares a candidate model against a *baseline*. In this chapter, we explain R^2 in three stages. First, we develop a working intuition of R^2 with several analogies. Second, we show in detail how to calculate R^2. Finally, we combine intuition and computation by interpreting the three key terms involved in calculating R^2.

R^2 is a ratio

R^2 is a ratio. To motivate our understanding of the ratio, we begin with a couple of analogies. The first example is drawn from the world of sports and the second from the world of finance. The point of the examples is to understand the numerator and the denominator of the ratio in R^2.

Our first example comes from basketball. Let's suppose that a basketball player averages 70 successful free-throw shots per 100, for a shooting percentage of 70%. We will call this the player's *baseline* performance. The player's *total gap* in performance is 30. Any improvements in performance will be evaluated against this gap in the baseline performance.

Let's suppose now that the athlete practices a new free-throw technique to improve their performance. As a result, performance improves from 70 to 80 successful shots per 100, bringing the shooting percentage up to 80%. The total gap has now decreased from 30 to 20. We can think of the new free-throw technique as a new model in machine learning. Since the model *lifts* the number of successful shots from 70 to 80, we will call the 10 additional shots the *model lift*.

We now have everything we need to calculate R^2 for the basketball player's new technique or "model." We can calculate R^2 for the new free-throw technique as:

$$R^2 = \frac{\text{model lift}}{\text{total gap}} = \frac{10}{30} = .33 = 33\%$$

It's important to note that the denominator contains a total. But the total is *not* the total number of free-throw shots (i.e., 100). Rather, it's the *total gap* (30) in the baseline performance. The numerator (*model lift*) counts the improvement (10) relative to the total gap.

As our example shows, R^2 tells us the relative improvement against the baseline model. R^2 is a number between 0 and 1, but it can also be reported as a percentage. From our knowledge of R^2 we can also calculate how much room remains for improvement. The *remaining gap* is .66 or 66%. It can be calculated by either subtracting R^2

from 1, or calculated directly as the ratio of the remaining gap to the total gap.

$$1 - R^2 = \frac{\text{remaining gap}}{\text{total gap}} = \frac{20}{30} = .66 = 66\%$$

In our second example, we will use R^2 to evaluate a company's financial performance. Let's suppose a company sets \$1M in revenue as its target for the coming year. The company's revenue last year was \$600K. Using last year's revenue as the baseline, the company projects a total gap of \$400K.

At this point, the company considers various strategies for closing the gap. The most promising is an advertisement campaign that is projected to increase revenue by \$200K. As a result, total sales would increase from the baseline of \$600K to \$800K. Once again, we can think of the advertisement campaign as analogous to a new machine learning model. The model lift of the advertising campaign is \$200K.

We are now ready to calculate R^2 for the advertising campaign:

$$R^2 = \frac{\text{model lift}}{\text{total gap}} = \frac{200K}{400K} = .50 = 50\%$$

Once again, we note that the denominator is not the total target budget, which is set at \$1M. The denominator is the *total gap* in the baseline model, which is \$400K. The numerator is the lift provided by the advertising campaign or the new model.

As before, we can also calculate the remaining gap percentage:

$$1 - R^2 = \frac{\text{remaining gap}}{\text{total gap}} = \frac{200K}{400K} = .50$$

The calculations and terminology for the two examples are summarized in Table 9.1.

Table 9.1: R^2 Terminology and various comparisons.

Category	Basketball	Sales	Terminology	Symbols
Target	100	1M		
Baseline	70	600K		
Total Gap	30	400K	SSTotal	$y - \bar{y}$
Model Lift	10	200K	SSRegression	$\hat{y} - \bar{y}$
Remaining Gap	20	200K	SSResiduals	$y - \hat{y}$
Model Lift ÷ Total Gap	.33	.50	R^2	
Remaining Gap ÷ Total Gap	.66	.50	$1 - R^2$	

R^2 characteristics

We pause to make some important observations about R^2 as a metric. First, R^2's value always ranges from 0 to 1. The least successful model has an R^2 of 0, while the most successful model has an R^2 of 1. Here, the analogy with revenue targets breaks down since it is conceivable that actual revenue can exceed targeted revenue. For our purposes, what's important is that the *total gap* in the baseline becomes the target for evaluating the performance of the new model.

Second, with any measurement, we need to be mindful of units. In the case of R^2, since actual and target values have the same units, the units cancel each other out. R^2 as a measurement, therefore, is dimensionless. This is advantageous since we don't have to worry about the units of our variables in order to estimate model accuracy. It doesn't matter, for example, whether we record revenue in dollars, euros, or yen when comparing models.

R^2 visualized

We now consider a visual example to solidify our intuition. Suppose we start with an empty cylindrical container, as shown in left panel of Figure 9.1. Using our earlier terminology, the size of the container is the total gap. Our goal is to fill the container all the way to the top. Each attempt to fill the container corresponds to a different machine learning model. In the middle and right panels of Figure 9.1, we see a container and two model attempts. R^2 for the first model is .7, since we were able to fill 70 % of the container. R^2 for the second model is .2, since we were able to fill only 20 %. We can conclude that the first model is better than the second, since we were able to fill more of the container.

Figure 9.1: R^2 can be used to compare models. Model 1 fills a greater percentage of the "container" than Model 2.

$$R^2 = \frac{volume_{filled}}{volume_{total}}$$

The first model is also better, since the proportion of unfilled container is smaller:

$$1 - R^2 = \frac{volume_{unfilled}}{volume_{total}}$$

9.3 R^2 – Computation

Armed with an intuitive understanding of R^2, let's now look at how it's calculated. We begin by introducing three formal terms:
-   Total Sum of Squares Total (SS_{total})
-   Residual Sum of Squares ($SS_{residual}$)
-   Regression Sum of Squares ($SS_{regression}$)

Let's first map the three terms to our examples.

SS_{total} corresponds to the size of the container. In our examples, we called it the *total gap* in the baseline model. It's the denominator in R^2. $SS_{regression}$ is the filled portion of the container. In our examples, we called it the *model lift*. It's the numerator in R^2. Finally, $SS_{residual}$ corresponds to the unfilled portion of the container. In our examples, we called it the *remaining gap*. Figure 9.2 shows the correspondence of each term with the container analogy.

Container

Total = SS_total

unfilled = SS_residual

filled = SS_regression

Figure 9.2: SS Total is the size of the container, SS Regression is the filled portion of the container, and SS Residual is the unfilled portion of the container.

Let's now turn to calculating R^2 using the three terms. In performing the calculations, we need to keep in mind three data points (Figure 9.3) in regression models and the distances between them. The first point is the actual or observed value (y). The second point is the predicted value ($\hat{y}$). The third point is the mean ($\bar{y}$) of the target variable.

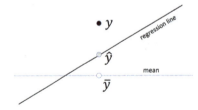

• y

regression line

$\hat{y}$

mean

$\bar{y}$

Figure 9.3: R^2 is calculated from three points. y is the actual or observed value. $\hat{y}$ is the predicted value. $\bar{y}$ is the mean of the observed values.

Residual Sum of Squares

We already know how to calculate $SS_{residual}$. It is calculated in terms of the distance of the actual point from the predicted point. It's the sum of the squares of the difference between the predicted point and the actual point.

$$SS_{residual} = \sum_{i=1}^{n}(y_i - \hat{y}_i)^2 \tag{9.1}$$

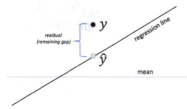

Figure 9.4: Sum of Squared Residuals is based on the distance of actual point from the predicted point.

Figure 9.4 shows that $SS_{residual}$ is based on the distance of the actual point to the predicted point on the regression line.

Total Sum of Squares

We calculate SS_{total} in terms of the distance of each observed value to the mean. In statistics, this is just the variance. SS_{total} measures the variance of the target variable. The greater the variance of our target variable, the larger the container. A large starting variance also means that the regression model has to account for, explain, and overcome a large beginning gap.

$$SS_{total} = \sum_{i=1}^{n}(y_i - \bar{y})^2 \tag{9.2}$$

Figure 9.5 illustrates that SS_{total} is based on the distance of each point to the mean line. The mean line is mean of the target values or the y variable.

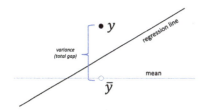

Figure 9.5: Sum of Squares Total is based on the distance of the actual point to the mean.

Regression Sum of Squares

Our third expression, $SS_{regression}$ can be calculated indirectly or directly. If we know SS_{total} and $SS_{Residual}$, it can be calculated as the difference between the two:

$$SS_{regression} = SS_{total} - SS_{residual}$$

The equation expresses the relationship between the three elements in our container analogy. The total volume of the container is the sum of the filled portion and the unfilled portion.

$SS_{regression}$ can also be calculated directly from the sum of squares of the difference between the regression line and the mean. The distance between regression line and the mean is also shown in Figure 9.6.

$$SS_{regression} = \sum_{i=1}^{n}(\hat{y}_i - \bar{y}_i)^2 \qquad (9.3)$$

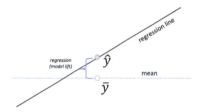

Figure 9.6: Sum of Squares Regression is based on the distance of predicted point to the mean.

9.3.1 Calculating R^2

We are now ready to calculate R^2. It is simply the ratio of $SS_{regression}$ and SS_{total}:

$$R^2 = \frac{SS_{regression}}{SS_{total}} \qquad (9.4)$$

R^2 can also be expressed alternatively as:

$$R^2 = 1 - \frac{SS_{residual}}{SS_{total}}$$

9.4 Interpreting R^2

We first developed an intuitive picture of R^2 based on a ratio of model lift compared to total gap. We then showed how to calculate it as the ratio of $SS_{regression}$ to SS_{total}. The remaining gap is $SS_{residual}$.

We now circle back and take a fresh look at the terms SS_{total}, $SS_{regression}$, and $SS_{residual}$ in light of our examples. We begin with SS_{total}. Why is it calculated as the distance of the actual point (y) to the mean ($\bar{y}$)? What is the significance of the mean? Why does it appear in our calculation of the baseline model?

Suppose we are in a room with fifty people. The exact number does not matter. It can be any n. Let's suppose that as a starting point we are given the heights of everyone in the room. Not knowing anything more than their heights, we are asked to predict the height of the next person who walks into the room. And the next person. And the next person. And so on. What would be a good model to make such predictions?

The most natural metric to use, of course, is the *mean* height of everyone already in the room. Lacking any further information, the mean is an excellent candidate for our baseline model. Whenever someone new steps into the room, we will predict their height based on the mean height of everyone already in the room. There are no differential predictions. We always predict the same height (i. e. the mean). This simple model might not be realistic or all that useful, but in the absence of further information it can serve as the baseline for evaluating improvements. The equation for the simple model is:

$$y = \bar{h}$$

We note that the equation is the equation for regression with only the intercept, $\beta_0 = \bar{h}$.

Before considering any improvements to the model, let's calculate the error in this simple model. In this case, the residual is the difference between the actual height (h) of an individual and the mean height ($\bar{h}$). As in the case of computing the error for a regression line, we will use sum of the squared errors rather than the absolute distance. The total error for this simple model then turns out to be:

$$\sum_{i=1}^{n}(y_i - \bar{y})^2$$

But this is what we have called the sum of squares total (SS_{total}).

Next, suppose we are able to obtain an additional piece of information about an individual who walks into the room. For example, what if we knew their weight? Can we predict the height of someone new walking into the room by knowing their weight? Moreover, will the prediction be an improvement of just using the mean height as in our simple baseline model?

The steps for answering the question is straightforward. We could try developing a simple linear regression model with weight as the feature variable and height as the target variable. Once we have completed the regression, we can calculate $SS_{residual}$. But what is $SS_{residual}$? It is the total error in the new model based on the calculation of the distance between the actual point and the model's prediction.

$$SS_{residual} = \sum_{i=1}^{n} (y_i - \hat{y}_i)^2$$

We are now ready to calculate R^2 for our example with heights. The denominator is the total gap using the mean height as the predictor in the baseline model. The numerator is the improvement that comes from using an additional variable (i. e., weight) to improve the prediction.

$$R^2 = \frac{\sum(\hat{y}_i - \bar{h})^2}{\sum(y_i - \bar{h})^2} = \frac{\sum(\hat{h}_i - \bar{h})^2}{\sum(h_i - \bar{h})^2}$$

In summary, R^2 compares two quantities.
–   The sum of squared errors from the regression model
–   The sum of squared errors from the baseline model.

In the case where there are no independent variables, the intercept is just the mean. In the baseline model, the predicted value for every case is the mean.

Finally, we note another important point about terminology. We stated earlier that R^2 is a number between 0 and 1. But sometimes it is also stated as a percentage. For example, a value of .32 for R^2 is equivalent to 32%. In statistics and machine learning, R^2 is used for model assessment and evaluation. But very often in the social sciences, one encounters R^2 as a metric for weighing the importance of independent variables. The independent variables in a particular model is said to "explain" X% of the variation in the dependent variable, where X is the value of R^2.

9.5 Summary

In this chapter, we began with restating MSE as a vital metric for evaluating a regression model. We then developed a complementary metric called R^2. R^2 is a ratio. The denominator in the ratio is the variance of the target variable. The variance is based on summing the squared distances of each point from the mean. The numerator in R^2 is the sum of the squared distances of each predicted value to the mean. The ratio represents an improvement in prediction relative to the baseline model based on the mean.

10 Model Assessment – Classification

In this chapter, we present some key metrics for evaluating classification models. Although our focus will be *binary classification*, the same techniques can be applied for *multiclass* or multinomial classification. We begin with *accuracy* as a crude first estimate. We then develop a more careful approach by using a *confusion matrix*. A confusion matrix is a contingency table which gives positive and negative matches for each class. The results of a confusion matrix are leveraged to develop a variety of metrics for evaluating classification models. Finally, we show how a Receiver Operating Characteristic (ROC) curve along with its Area Under the Curve (AUC) can display the tradeoffs inherent in classification algorithms.

> **Key Idea 1.** *Accuracy* is the simplest metric for evaluating classification models. It is defined as the ratio of correctly classified cases over total cases.
>
> **Key Idea 2.** Accuracy can be highly misleading in the cases where the data is *imbalanced*.
>
> **Key Idea 3.** A confusion matrix is a $N \times N$ table where each row represents a category and each column represents the prediction.
>
> **Key Idea 4.** An ROC (Receiver Operating Characteristic) curve is a graphical plot for visualizing the performance of a binary classifier. It tracks both the true positive rate and false positive rate for various threshold settings. The corresponding AUC (Area Under the Curve) provides a single aggregated metric for evaluating performance.

10.1 Accuracy

Let's start with a simple example. Suppose we are developing a classification model where we want to predict fraudulent transactions. We record 0 for a non-fraudulent transaction and 1 for a fraudulent transaction. Accuracy is simply the ratio of correct predictions to total predictions.

$$\text{Accuracy} = \frac{\text{correct predictions}}{\text{total predictions}}$$

For example, Figure 10.1 displays the accuracy computation for ten predictions. In this case, the accuracy score is $\frac{7}{10} = .7$.

We pause to observe that accuracy as a metric doesn't distinguish between categories. In other words, a match is a match whether the predicted and actual are fraudulent transactions (1s) or non-fraudulent (0s). Accuracy also does not distinguish be-

Actual	0	0	1	0	0	1	0	0	0	0
Predicted	0	0	0	1	0	1	1	0	0	0
	✓	✓			✓	✓		✓	✓	✓

Figure 10.1: Accuracy is the ratio of correct predictions to total predictions.

https://doi.org/10.1515/9781501505737-010

tween the case where actual is 1 and predicted 0, and the case where actual is 0 and predicted 1.

This can be highly misleading whenever there is a large imbalance among the classes. This is not just a theoretical scenario. It turns out that in many practical examples there is often an imbalance in representation among the classes. For example, the occurrence of a covid-infected individual in a random sample is much less frequent than a non-infected individual. The appearance of a terrorist at a screening checkpoint is much less frequent than a non-terrorist.

Let's suppose that our goal is to predict fraudulent credit card transactions. Let's further suppose that only 1 out of 1,000 transactions is fraudulent. This suggests a *trivial model* where we classify or predict *all* transactions as non-fraudulent. Despite the fact that the model never predicts a single fraudulent transaction correctly, it is 99.9 % accurate! Clearly something is wrong. When one, or more, category dominates the others, accuracy alone can be a highly misleading metric for evaluating classification models. This leads us to the idea of a confusion matrix where we track success and failure separately for each class.

10.2 Confusion Matrix

The primary method for evaluating model performance for classification is the confusion matrix. We begin with a simple picture of how a confusion matrix works.

Imagine a fisherman. The fisherman's goal is to catch tuna, but not to trap dolphins. We can think of the fisherman's fishnet as a classification model. The perfect net catches all tuna but avoids all dolphins. Let's suppose that in the area there are 100 tuna and 14 dolphins. The perfect fishnet captures all 100 tuna and spares all 14 dolphins. The most imperfect fishnet traps all 14 dolphins and captures 0 tuna. In practice, the result is likely to be somewhere in between. The fishing vessel returns with the catch shown in Figure 10.2. The fishnet caught 80 tuna but, unfortunately, trapped 8 dolphins.

Given the results, we can set up the confusion matrix as a 2×2 table shown in Figure 10.3.

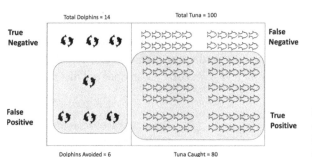

Figure 10.2: The fishing net caught 80 out of the 100 tuna. It also inadvertently captured 8 out of the 14 dolphins.

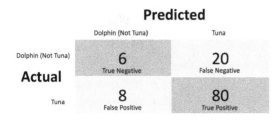

Figure 10.3: A Confusion Matrix records correct and incorrect predictions for all categories.

Based on the confusion matrix, we define four key terms: True Positive, True Negative, False Positive, and False Negative. In the language of prediction, both True Positives and True Negatives are correct predictions, while False Positives and False Negatives are incorrect predictions.

- True Positive (TP): The number of tuna captured
- True Negative (TN): The number of dolphins spared
- False Positive (FP): The number of dolphins trapped
- False Negative (FN): The number of tuna missed

Figure 10.4 shows the general form of a confusion matrix. The top left quadrant (True Negative) and the bottom right quadrant (True Positive) are *True* because the predictions match the actual values. The top right quadrant (False Negative) and bottom left quadrant (False Positive) are *False* because the predictions don't match the actual values.

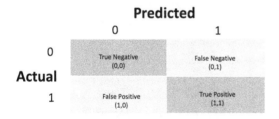

Figure 10.4: A general confusion matrix records True Negatives, True Positives, False Negatives, and False Positives.

In the world of epidemiology and statistics, False Positives are also known as Type I errors while False Negatives are known as Type II errors.

10.3 Precision and Recall

Once we have a confusion matrix and a definition of the four basic terms (TN, FP, FN, TP), we can pose a series of analytics questions about the effectiveness of our classification model. Instead of tuna and dolphins, let's consider a realistic example about predictions. The confusion chart in Figure 10.5 reports statistics associated with a Covid test. The test predicts who has Covid and who does not. Let's assume that the total number of individual tested is 1,000. Of the total number, 900 do not have Covid and 100 have Covid. Let's suppose that the test identified 85 individuals as having Covid. Let's now pose a series of questions about the test.

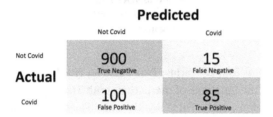

Predicted

	Not Covid	Covid
Not Covid	**900** True Negative	**15** False Negative
Actual		
Covid	**100** False Positive	**85** True Positive

Figure 10.5: Confusion Matrix for a Covid test.

Accuracy

– Q1: *How accurate was the test (or predictive model)?*

We already know how to calculate accuracy. It's the number of successful predictions. But using the terminology of the confusion matrix, we can calculate Accuracy as:

$$\frac{TP + TN}{Total} = \frac{85 + 900}{1000} = .985$$

The test is highly accurate. However, we observe that the dataset is highly imbalanced. The number of individuals with Covid is small compared to those who don't have Covid.

Recall

– Q2: *What percentage of Covid cases did the test identify correctly?*

The answer to this question is referred to as Recall and it is calculated as:

$$\frac{TP}{TP + FN} = \frac{85}{85 + 15} = .85$$

Of the total 100 cases, the test successfully identified 85. Recall is also known as Sensitivity, hit rate, and the True Positive Rate (TPR).

Precision

– Q3: *What percentage of the items identified as Covid was actually Covid?*

The answer to this question is called Precision and it is calculated as:

$$\frac{TP}{TP + FP} = \frac{85}{85 + 100} = .46$$

A low Precision number is equivalent to having a large number of False Positives.

Revisiting Accuracy

Let's return to our example of fraudulent transactions, where only one in a thousand transactions is fraudulent. In our trivial model, we *always* predicted the majority category (i. e. not-fraudulent) and achieved an accuracy score of 99.9 %. But given the confusion matrix, the Recall score for the trivial model is 0.

In the Covid case, let's change the numbers and see how it changes the Recall and Precision numbers. Let's suppose that out of the 100 Covid cases, the test successfully identified 99. However, the number of false positives was 200. The accuracy rate is still high at 89 %. Recall jumps to 99 %. However, Precision falls to 33 %. Again, low Precision means a high number of False Positives.

10.4 ROC/AUC Curve

With so many metrics available, it can be confusing to decide which metric to use. Fortunately, a summary plot called the Receiving Operating Characteristic (ROC) curve, along with its Area Under the Curve (AUC) provides a shorthand way of gauging the overall effectiveness of the model.

An ROC curve (Figure 10.6) plots the True Positive Rate (TPR) against the False Positive Rate (FPT) at various threshold settings. The y-axis is TPR, which is the same as Recall. The x-axis is the FPT. The False Positive Rate tells us the proportion of the negative class which was incorrectly identified by the classifier. In our Covid example, the negative class are people without Covid. Out of a 1000 non-Covid cases, 100 were incorrectly identified as having Covid. Therefore, the False Positive Rate is .1 or 10 %. The True Positive Rate was .85 or 85 %. In general, we want low FPR (left side of x-axis) and high TPR (top of y-axis). A random classifier which randomly guesses or predicts hit, or miss, will fall on the diagonal. An extremely poor predictor will be worse than random.

An ROC curve is generated by calculating and then plotting TPR against FPR at various threshold settings. What is a threshold setting? Although binary classifiers predict a 1 or 0, the prediction is based on a probability. The default threshold is set at 0.5, meaning that a prediction with a probability greater than 0.5 is classified as 1, otherwise as 0. Both the confusion matrix and the classification report are generated from the default threshold. On the other hand, an ROC runs through a variety of

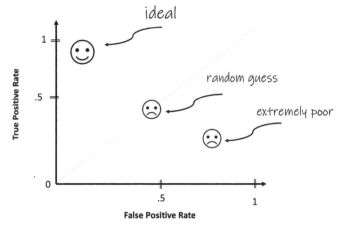

Figure 10.6: An ROC curve is visual way of representing the tradeoff between True Positives and False Positives. The aim is to attain a high True Positive Rate and a low False Positive Rate.

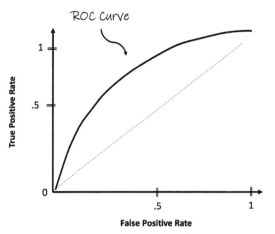

Figure 10.7: ROC Curve.

probability thresholds from 0 to 1 and generates TPR and FPR based on the specific threshold. They are then plotted as the ROC curve, as shown in Figure 10.7.

Once we have the ROC curve, we can calculate the area under the curve. A larger area means a more useful model and higher prediction accuracy. The Area Under Curve (AUC) metric ranges from 0 to 1. A random-guess predictor is the area under the diagonal line, which has the value of .5. The AUC is the shaded region under the ROC Curve, as shown in Figure 10.8.

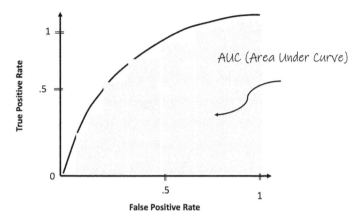

Figure 10.8: The area under an ROC Curve (AUC) is a single metric for evaluating classification models. It ranges from 0 to 1. The higher the score, the better the classification model.

10.5 Summary

In this chapter, we began by showing how to calculate accuracy for a classification model. We argued that accuracy can be highly misleading in the case of imbalanced data and should not be relied upon as the sole metric for classification models. We then presented a confusion matrix, which records the hits and misses for both positive and negative cases. We then defined a number of metrics based on the confusion matrix. Finally, we presented a summary metric called Receiver Operating Characteristic (ROC) curve and its corresponding Area Under the Curve (AUC). The better the classification model, the higher the value for AUC, which ranges from 0 to 1.

Part III: **Machine Learning II**

11 Multiple Linear Regression – Concept

In this chapter, we begin our study of multiple linear regression (MLR). In simple linear regression our aim was to predict a single target variable from a single feature variable. In simple linear regression, both target and feature variables were *continuous*. With multiple linear regression our aim is to increase *predictive power* by using *multiple* feature variables.

Key Idea 1. In MLR, *multiple* feature variables are used to predict a *single* target variable.

Key Idea 2. In MLR, the target variable is continuous while the feature variables can be either continuous or discrete.

Key Idea 3. In MLR, the target variable is a *linear combination* of the feature variables.

Key Idea 4. A MLR model, similar to SLR, minimizes the sum of the squares of the residuals.

Key Idea 5. In MLR, each *regression coefficient* indicates the amount of *change* in the target variable based on a *unit change* in the feature variable, while *controlling* for the other feature variables.

Key Idea 6. In MLR, the number of *model parameters* is the number of feature variables + 1.

11.1 Bird's Eye View

The real world is a world of causation. A virus causes disease. Capital investment causes company growth. Force causes acceleration. Meanwhile, machine learning models inhabit the shadowy world of correlations. At first glance, this appears to be a major drawback. Science, after all, not only describes *how* things are, but explains *why* things are the way they are. A chasm separates machine learning as correlation from science as causation.

Here multiple linear regression comes to a partial rescue. In this chapter, we will call upon multiple linear regression to do double duty. Our primary goal is still prediction: we can *predict y*, without knowing what *causes y*. We can increase predictive power by increasing the number of features in our model. But our secondary goal is to anticipate causal analysis. We will see that MLR is a powerful tool for making predictions, but it also provides an initial glimpse into the structure of causality. Although causal analysis is outside the scope of this book, a solid understanding of multiple regression provides an essential background for later study of causality. Multiple regression also provides a foundation for understanding the structure of deep learning models.

Accordingly, we begin our study of MLR by assuming a highly *simplified causal picture* of the world. We wish to understand how some effect *e* arises. Our simplified causal picture makes four basic assumptions. Our first assumption states that for any effect *e*, there are multiple *possible* causes: $c_1, c_2, \ldots, c_n$. This first assumption, as illus-

https://doi.org/10.1515/9781501505737-011

trated in Figure 11.1, conforms to our ordinary notion of causality. A one-to-one cause-effect relationship is rare. A many-to-one cause-effect relationship is more common. In statistics, a possible cause is also referred to as a *covariate*. Occasionally, we will make use of this alternative terminology.

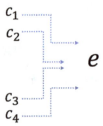

Figure 11.1: Effects usually have multiple causes.

Our second assumption states that each cause acts *independently* of the others. In the real world, this assumption is frequently violated. Causes quite often conspire together to bring about an effect. Two criminals work together to rob a bank. Several musicians, along with a conductor, perform a symphony. Genes and environment work in tandem to produce traits or phenotypes. Models that take into account interactions between causes are called *additive* or *interactive models*. But in our simplified world, we will assume that causes are entirely solitary creatures, acting upon the effect wholly independently of other causes.

Our third assumption states that causes *vary* in their contribution to the effect. Some causes play a stronger role while others play a weaker role in bringing about an effect. I am sad today because it is raining *and* I lost my favorite book. What is the greater cause of sadness? Is it the fact that it is raining, my having lost a prized book, or some combination of both?

We can capture the strength of the cause by associating a multiplicative weight (w). The causes that contribute more to bringing about the effect have higher weights, and those which contribute less have lower weights. The multiplicative weight of each cause is illustrated in Figure 11.2.

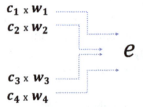

Figure 11.2: Causes vary in their contribution to bringing about an effect. This can be captured in linear models by using weights.

Our final assumption states the *overall* effect is simply the weighted sum or *linear combination* of the causes. A linear combination is a type of aggregation. Instead of taking a simple sum, we calculate a weighted sum. In mathematics, a linear combination is constructed from a set of terms by multiplying each term by a constant and adding the results. In our case, the terms are the variables representing the causes and the constants are the corresponding weights.

$$\textbf{effect} = w_1 c_1 + w_2 c_2 + \cdots w_n c_n$$

To complete the picture, we also add a bias term b to the weighted sum. As we saw in simple linear regression, the bias term is also known as the intercept. It is included to accommodate instances where the value of the dependent variable might be non-zero even when the values of all the independent variables are zero.

$$\textbf{effect} = w_1 c_1 + w_2 c_2 + \cdots w_n c_n + b$$

If we rewrite the equation using standard variables x and y, where x stands for cause and y stands for effect, and weights are expressed with β, then we arrive at the fundamental equation for multiple regression:

MLR Equation: $\quad y = \beta_0 + \beta_1 x_1 + \beta_2 x_2 + \cdots \beta_n x_n$ $\qquad\qquad$ (11.1)

The MLR equation elegantly summarizes the four assumptions. Conceptually, we think of the effect simply as the weighted sum of the contributions of the causes. This approach to modeling has several advantages. First, we are able to *separate* out each cause and examine its specific contribution to the effect. As a practical matter, we want to understand *that* a cause influences some effect. But we also want to understand *how much* that cause influences the effect. This is achieved with the weight or coefficient in the multiple linear regression equation.

Second, multiple regression models are interpretable. As we saw in the chapters on SLR, interpretable models generate a prediction, but we can also peer inside the "black box" to examine how the prediction is generated. Transparency is a critical aim of model development, especially when our models have to be explained to stakeholders.

Third, multiple regression belongs to the family of *linear models*. Why is this important? Linear models have well understood mathematical properties that make them ideal for a variety of use cases.

In summary, we have explicated multiple regression in two ways. From the standpoint of prediction, the target variable y is a linear combination of the feature variables $x_1, x_2, \ldots, x_n$. From the standpoint of causality, the effect is a linear combination of the causes.

11.2 Multiple Regression Workflow

Given an overview of multiple linear regression, we are now ready to put it into practice. The process of modeling using multiple regression is analogous to solving a murder mystery. How does a detective go about solving a murder?

Detective Jane Marple appears at the scene of a crime. First, she poses questions and collects data. Next, she develops a preliminary list of suspects. In some cases, multiple suspects might be involved in the crime. Next, Detective Marple investigates the relationship of each suspect to the victim and the suspects to each other. Next, Detective Marple crosses off, by a process of elimination, some of the suspects from the list. Next, she frames an argument detailing the contribution of each remaining suspect to the crime. Finally, arrests are made and a case is brought forward for trial. These steps need not occur, of course, linearly. But they constitute some of the essential steps in solving a murder mystery.

The workflow in multiple regression proceeds in an analogous fashion.
- **Step 1**: Identify the feature and target variables. (*hypothesis formation*)
- **Step 2**: Understand descriptive properties of the feature and target variables. (*exploratory data analysis*)
- **Step 3**: Evaluate the correlations among the feature and target variables. (*statistical analysis*)
- **Step 4**: Evaluate the statistical significance of the feature variables. (*statistical analysis, regression analysis*)
- **Step 5**: Estimate the weights or coefficients for each of the feature variables. (*regression analysis*)
- **Step 6**: Evaluate the model. (*regression analysis*)

11.3 Case Study: Does Sleep Improve Academic Performance?

We are now ready to apply our knowledge of multiple linear regression with a case study. Our goal in the case study is to predict exam performance. What factors affect academic achievement? Can academic achievement be improved? If so, how?

Analytic Question: Does more sleep improve final exam grade?

In the context of machine learning, can we predict a student's final exam score if we know how much sleep they received the night before? Of course, we could apply simple linear regression. The regression would then use *sleep* as the feature variable and final exam *score* as the target variable. In the case study, we want to understand the role of sleep, but we also want to consider other factors that might affect final exam grade.

Identify predictor and target variables

As part of the research design, we hypothesize that a number of variables, along with sleep, are likely to affect exam performance. Which additional variables? Certainly, *student ability* is likely to play a role. Better students perform better than poorer students. The quality of the *instructional environment* is also likely to matter. A student is more likely to learn in a supportive environment. Also, the *amount of time* a student studies or practices for the exam is also likely to play a role in improving the final exam grade.

We have developed a preliminary list of possible causes, covariates, or "suspects" of academic performance. We now come across our first hurdle. Each of our variables have to be measurable. Measuring the quality of the instructional environment, for example, is complex. It's not easily measurable, since it is a function of teacher quality, curriculum quality, the time allocated for instruction, and so on. In such complex cases, we can sometimes resort to a useful stratagem: we introduce a *proxy variable*. A proxy is something that stands in for something else. Since instructional quality is difficult to measure, we can try employing *parental income* as a proxy. In our study, we will use parental income as a *proxy* for the quality of instructional environment. Our supposition is that wealthier students will have access to more instructional resources and opportunities than poorer students. Proxy variables can be handy but they should always be used guardedly, since we might be smuggling in unknown assumptions.

Figure 11.3: Some possible causes of final exam grade.

Along with sleep and parental income, we will include two other variables in our study. The first is study time: the number of hours a student spent studying for the exam. Second, we include each student's incoming grade point average (GPA). Here again, we are resorting to a proxy variable. Student ability, which should influence academic performance, is once again complex and difficult to measure. We hypothesize that GPA can serve as a proxy for student ability. Figure 11.3 summarizes the prediction structure for the multiple linear regression case study.

We have settled, therefore, on four independent variables or features for our multiple regression model: *Sleep*, *Time*, *GPA*, and *Income*. Through multiple regression, we aim to predict final exam grade based on these four feature variables.

Exploratory Data Analysis

The researchers perform the study and come back with data for each of the four feature variables and the target variable.

Dataset

The dataset contains 2,077 observations with 6 columns. Table 11.1 shows a sample of the data collected from the study. The first column is an index mapped to a unique student. The next four columns are the feature, or predictor variables. The final column is the target variable. *GPA* is the student's incoming grade point average. *Income* is the student's family income. *Sleep* is the hours of sleep the student received the night before the final exam. *Time* is the number of hours the student studied for the final exam. *Grade* is the final score the student received on the final exam.

Table 11.1: Sample data for academic performance.

ID	GPA	Income	Sleep	Time	Grade
0	2.9	82461	6.5	47	77
1	3.7	61113	6.2	47	94
2	2.8	63632	6.2	39	69
3	2.0	66854	7.2	49	81
4	2.8	82721	5.5	49	78

Distribution

Figure 11.4 shows the distribution of each of the variables in the form of a histogram. It is apparent that the distribution for each is normal. While this is by no means a requirement for predictive models, it's important to understand beforehand the distribution of each of the key variables.

Figure 11.5 displays the final exam grade distribution, which also is more or less normally distributed.

Summary Statistics

Figure 11.6 displays summary descriptive statistics for each of the variables. For example, family income has a low of approximately $28K and a high of $129K. Mean income is $75K with a standard deviation of $15K.

Correlations

Figure 11.7 displays correlations among the variables in the form of a heatmap. The final row shows the correlations of the target variable (*Grade*) to each of the feature variables (*GPA, Income, Sleep*, and *Time*). The final grade correlates most strongly with

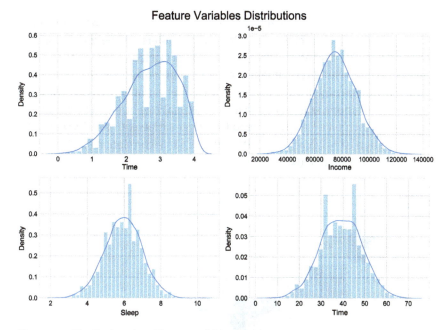

Figure 11.4: Distribution plot of feature variables.

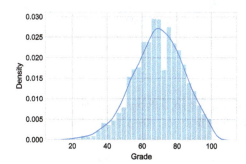

Figure 11.5: Distribution plot of final exam grade.

	GPA	Income	Sleep	Time	Grade
count	2,077.0	2,077.0	2,077.0	2,077.0	2,077.0
mean	2.7	75,282.6	6.0	39.1	69.2
std	0.8	15,264.4	1.0	9.4	14.5
min	0.2	27,952.0	2.5	7.0	19.0
25%	2.2	65,073.0	5.3	32.0	60.0
50%	2.8	75,040.0	6.0	39.0	70.0
75%	3.3	85,492.0	6.7	46.0	79.0
max	4.0	128,655.0	10.1	70.0	100.0

Figure 11.6: Summary statistics of feature and target variables.

the amount of time studying and weakly with income. The first four rows report correlations between each of the predictor variables with the others. All the correlations are weak. This is important to bear in mind since a strong correlation among the predictor variables is likely to violate our independence assumption, namely that the feature variables act independently of one another on the target variable. We will review the importance of correlations later in the chapter. The final row of the heatmap shows the correlation of each predictor variable to the target variable, *Grade*. *Time* has the strongest correlation (0.64). *Sleep* and *GPA* have the same correlation (0.45). *Income* shows a very weak correlation (0.012).

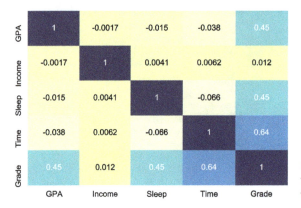

Figure 11.7: Heatmap of correlations shows the correlations of all the variables.

Run Regression – Round One

We are now ready to run the regression. Before doing so, let's review where we are. Our aim is to predict final exam grade based on four features: sleep, study time, parental income, and incoming grade point average. Our primary research question is whether sleep influences academic performance, particularly for the final exam.

The general form of the regression estimate is:

$$\hat{y} = \hat{\beta}_0 + \hat{\beta}_1 x_1 + \hat{\beta}_2 x_2 + \cdots \hat{\beta}_n x_n$$

In the equation, $\hat{y}$ is the model estimate of the target variable or what we are trying to predict. The feature variables are represented by $x_1 \ldots x_n$. The coefficients $\hat{\beta}_1, \hat{\beta}_2, \ldots \hat{\beta}_n$ represent estimates of the weights corresponding to the feature variables. The term $\hat{\beta}_0$ represents an estimate of the intercept.

We observe that the number of parameters for the model is the list of βs, which is the number of feature variables + 1. In our case study, the number of parameters, therefore, is 5.

For our case study, the specific form of the regression equation is:

$$\text{Grade} = \hat{\beta}_0 + \hat{\beta}_1 \times \textbf{GPA} + \hat{\beta}_2 \times \textbf{Practice} + \hat{\beta}_3 \times \textbf{Sleep} + \hat{\beta}_4 \times \textbf{Income}$$

Regression Summary

When we run the regression, we obtain the results shown in Figure 11.8. The summary contains a lot of information and seems forbidding at first glance. We focus on three items: *p-values* as reported in the column **P > |t|**, values of the coefficients as listed in the **coef** column, and the value of *R-squared*.

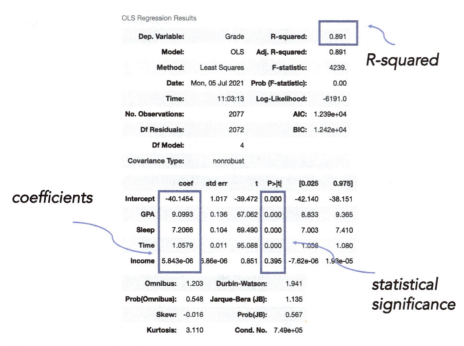

Figure 11.8: Summary of Multiple Linear Regression, Round One.

Statistical Significance

What is *p-value*? Conceptually it tells us how confident we can be about the estimates of the values of the coefficients. The *p-values* for GPA, *Sleep*, and *Time* are less than .05. Therefore, we interpret the result as statistically significant. The *p-value* for *Income*, however, is much greater than .05, the actual value being .395. This means that the estimate of the coefficient for *Income* is not statistically significant.

What does this mean practically? Going back to our analogy of solving a murder mystery, it means that the statistical evidence associating *Income* with exam *Grade* is weak. The two items are not likely to be related.

Coefficients

Now let's look at the estimated values for the coefficients. The item to notice is the extremely small value of the coefficient for *Income*. The value of the coefficient for *Income* is written in scientific notation, which we can rewrite as (.000006) after rounding.

We now have two reasons for throwing out *Income* from our analysis. First, the result for *Income* is not statistically significant. Second, the weight of *Income* seems to be negligible. (We add a note of caution in interpreting sizes of coefficients. It depends entirely on the scale of measurement. In the next chapter on theory, we provide an alternative way of developing the coefficients based on standardization.)

R-squared

The regression summary also displays the R-squared value. In this case, the R-squared value is 0.89, which indicates a very good fit. We discuss R-squared in detail in Chapter 9.

Run Regression – Round Two

Based on our first regression analysis, we eliminate *Income* as a predictor from our model and run the regression again. The new results are shown in Figure 11.9. This time, all the feature variables are statistically significant: the *p-values* are all less than .05. We can now look at the coefficients and be confident that the estimates are correct. The value for R-squared also remains robust.

The Regression Equation

Given the values of the regression coefficients, we can write the regression equation as:

$$\text{Grade} = -39.7 + 9.10 \times \textbf{GPA} + 7.21 \times \textbf{Sleep} + 1.06 \times \textbf{Time}$$

From the regression equation we can easily predict scores based on any combination of values for *GPA*, *Sleep* and *Time* practiced. For example, a student with an incoming GPA of 3.0, who sleeps for 7 hours, and has practiced for 50 hours can expect a score of 91 on their final exam.

$$\textbf{Grade} = -39.7 + 9.10 \times (3.0) + 7.21 \times (7) + 1.06 \times (50) = 91$$

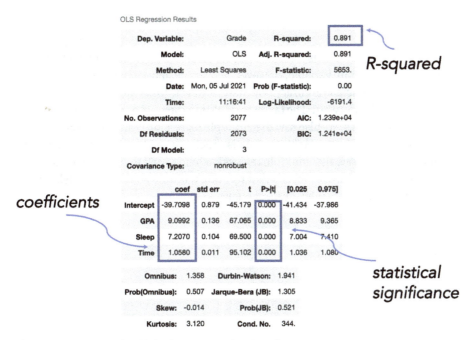

coefficients

R-squared

statistical significance

OLS Regression Results

Dep. Variable:	Grade	R-squared:	0.891	
Model:	OLS	Adj. R-squared:	0.891	
Method:	Least Squares	F-statistic:	5653.	
Date:	Mon, 05 Jul 2021	Prob (F-statistic):	0.00	
Time:	11:16:41	Log-Likelihood:	-6191.4	
No. Observations:	2077	AIC:	1.239e+04	
Df Residuals:	2073	BIC:	1.241e+04	
Df Model:	3			
Covariance Type:	nonrobust			

	coef	std err	t	P>|t|	[0.025	0.975]
Intercept	-39.7098	0.879	-45.179	0.000	-41.434	-37.986
GPA	9.0992	0.136	67.065	0.000	8.833	9.365
Sleep	7.2070	0.104	69.500	0.000	7.004	7.410
Time	1.0580	0.011	95.102	0.000	1.036	1.080

Omnibus:	1.358	Durbin-Watson:	1.941
Prob(Omnibus):	0.507	Jarque-Bera (JB):	1.305
Skew:	-0.014	Prob(JB):	0.521
Kurtosis:	3.120	Cond. No.	344.

Figure 11.9: Summary of Multiple Linear Regression, Round Two.

11.4 Interpreting the Regression Equation

We can interpret the regression coefficients as follows: For each unit of increase in GPA, final exam score increases on average by 9.10 points; each additional hour of sleep increases final exam score by 7.21 points; and one hour of additional study time leads to a 1.06 point gain on the final exam.

It appears that *GPA* leads to the biggest gains. However, we have to be careful because our variables have different units. As is, the coefficients are not comparable in terms of their influence on the outcome variable. However, there is a way to make the coefficients comparable. We look at the topic of *standardizing* coefficients in regression in the next chapter on theory.

We make another observation of practical significance. Some independent variables can't be changed. *GPA* is the incoming grade for the student. It can't be changed by the student during the course. By contrast, both *Sleep* and study *Time* are *actionable*. This means that an instructor can provide feedback to students *during the course*. What the study shows is that there are clear benefits to sleeping more the night before and studying consistently during the duration of the semester. Not only are there benefits, but we have precisely quantified the gains through multiple regression.

11.5 Summary

Simple linear regression was a useful starting point for predicting a target variable based on a single feature variable. However, in practice, most models require multiple features to gain sufficient accuracy. We saw, however, that extending simple linear regression is straightforward. The target variable is expressed as a linear combination of the feature variables. We also saw that multiple regression is advantageous because of its high degree of interpretability. This is crucial for getting buy-in among stake holders. Finally, we saw that multiple regression lends itself to thinking of the world in terms of cause-effect. This means that running multiple regression models can be a good prelude for a more robust causal analysis.

12 Multiple Linear Regression – Theory

In the previous chapter, we showed how multiple linear regression (MLR) uses multiple features to predict a continuous outcome. In this chapter, we discuss some key topics for interpreting MLR models. We begin by discussing *standardized coefficients*, also known as *beta coefficients* or *beta weights*. By comparing standardized coefficients, we can get an idea of which feature variables are more important than others in influencing the outcome variable. Next, we provide a modest checklist of regression diagnostics. Machine learning and statistics algorithms estimate values of the parameters based on a set of assumptions. The assumptions should be cross-checked before the model enters production.

Key Idea 1. MLR performed on an original dataset yields unstandardized coefficients. In order to compare the influence of the feature variables on the target variable, regression variables have to be *standardized*. The most common method for standardization is conversion to *z-scores*, which puts everything into a common metric of standard deviation units.

Key Idea 2. MLR assumes that the target variable y is *linearly* related to each of the feature variables x.

Key Idea 3. MLR assumes that the error terms are *normally distributed*.

Key Idea 4. MLR assumes the absence of *extreme multicollinearity* among the feature variables.

Key Idea 5. MLR assumes *homoscedasticity*, namely that the residuals or error terms in the regression have *constant variance*.

12.1 Standardized Coefficients

In the previous chapter, we saw that the equation for MLR is a linear combination of the predictors and coefficients:

$$\hat{y} = \hat{\beta}_0 + \hat{\beta}_1 x_1 + \hat{\beta}_2 x_2 + \cdots \hat{\beta}_n x_n$$

In the case of SLR, there are only two parameters: $\hat{\beta}_0$ and $\hat{\beta}_1$. The aim of regression is to estimate the value of the two parameters. In the case of MLR, there are $n+1$ parameters, where n is the number of features. The additional parameter is the intercept, $\hat{\beta}_0$.

We saw in the previous chapter that regression discovers or learns specific values for the coefficients. We then plug in specific values of the coefficients to arrive at the model. We then make predictions based on the model.

The case study for MLR, for example, used *three* feature variables to predict final exam score. Regression yielded the following estimates for the coefficients: $\hat{\beta}_0 = -39.7$, $\hat{\beta}_1 = 9.10$, $\hat{\beta}_2 = 7.21$, $\hat{\beta}_2 = 1.06$. Plugging in the values of the coefficients, the regression

https://doi.org/10.1515/9781501505737-012

equation was then expressed as:

$$\textbf{Grade} = -39.7 + 9.10 \times \textbf{GPA} + 7.21 \times \textbf{Sleep} + 1.06 \times \textbf{Time}$$

We then interpreted the regression equation as stating that for one unit increase in *GPA*, we can expect an average increase of 9.10 points on the final exam; one hour of additional *Sleep* leads on average to an additional 7.21 points; and an additional hour of *Time* leads to a 1.06 point increase.

Let's pause now and consider an important question. Which variable influences exam score the most? Do the coefficients allow us to rank the influence? Since $\hat{\beta}$ for *GPA* is higher than that of *Time* and *Sleep*, does this mean that *GPA* has the greatest effect on outcome? It would seem so, since we indicated that coefficients stand for weights and the largest weight is associated with *GPA*.

Although this line of reasoning seems plausible, it is fallacious. We can't interpret the regression coefficients straightforwardly as weights. Why? Because the variables each carry their own unit of measurement. When two variables have different units of measurement, they can't be compared as is. Two feet, for example, is not greater than one meter.

Standard scores (*z-scores*)

How can we determine which feature variable has the greatest influence on the outcome or variable? The way to proceed is to *standardize* the units. In statistics, a common approach for standardizing units is to use *z-scores*. A *z-score* is also called a standard score. It tells us the number of standard deviations a raw score falls above or below the mean. The *z-score* of the *i*th point among a set of points is calculated by subtracting the mean and then dividing the difference by the standard deviation. A point's *z-score* is that point's distance in standard deviations from the mean.

$$z_i = \frac{x_i - \mu}{\sigma}$$

In order to obtain *standardized coefficients*, we have to transform or standardize the data so that it is expressed as *z-scores*. Figure 12.1 compares the variable *Time* before and after scaling to *z-scores*. Before scaling, the values of the variable range approximately from 0 to 60. After scaling, the values range approximately from –3 to 3.

Regression with standardized coefficients

Once we have scaled the variables, we can rerun the regression to obtain standardized coefficients for the case study. Figure 12.2 is a summary report of the regression with

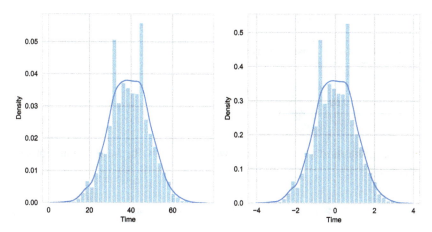

Figure 12.1: Standardizing a variable (e. g., *Time*) changes the units, but not the properties of the distribution.

OLS Regression Results

Dep. Variable:	Grade	R-squared:	0.891
Model:	OLS	Adj. R-squared:	0.891
Method:	Least Squares	F-statistic:	5653.
Date:	Mon, 05 Jul 2021	Prob (F-statistic):	0.00
Time:	11:46:18	Log-Likelihood:	-644.68
No. Observations:	2077	AIC:	1297.
Df Residuals:	2073	BIC:	1320.
Df Model:	3		
Covariance Type:	nonrobust		

	coef	std err	t	P>|t|	[0.025	0.975]
Intercept	-3.417e-16	0.007	-4.71e-14	1.000	-0.014	0.014
GPA	0.4866	0.007	67.065	0.000	0.472	0.501
Sleep	0.5050	0.007	69.500	0.000	0.491	0.519
Time	0.6914	0.007	95.102	0.000	0.677	0.706

Omnibus:	1.358	Durbin-Watson:	1.941
Prob(Omnibus):	0.507	Jarque-Bera (JB):	1.305
Skew:	-0.014	Prob(JB):	0.521
Kurtosis:	3.120	Cond. No.	1.08

Figure 12.2: Multiple linear regression summary with standardized coefficients.

standardized coefficients. The standardized coefficients are listed in Table 12.1. We also list the unstandardized coefficients for comparison.

We now have a basis for comparing the weights or influence of *GPA*, *Time*, and *Sleep*. Studying has the greatest benefit, *Sleep* and *GPA* are both the same at about

Table 12.1: A comparison of standardized and unstandardized coefficients.

Variable	Standardized Coeff	Unstandardized Coeff
GPA	0.49	9.10
Sleep	0.51	7.20
Time	0.69	1.06

30 % lower. Using standardized coefficients, we can also rewrite the MLR equation for the case study as:

$$\text{Grade} = 0.49 \times \textbf{GPA} + 0.51 \times \textbf{Sleep} + 0.69 \times \textbf{Time}$$

As the summary report shows in Figure 12.2, the intercept is no longer statistically significant, and its value, in any case, is close to 0. Therefore, we have left it out of the MLR equation.

Interpreting standardized coefficients

How do we interpret the regression equation using standardized coefficients? The common unit for standardized coefficients is standard deviations. For one standard deviation (**sd**) increase in *GPA*, there is on average .49 standard deviation increase in exam grade; for one standard deviation increase in *Sleep*, there is on average .51 standard deviation increase in exam grade; and, one standard deviation change in study *Time*, there is on average .69 standard deviation increase.

We note a couple of additional points on interpreting standardized coefficients. Since the concept of *z-score* is technical, non-standardized coefficients are likely to be more readily understood by the business and non-technical audiences. However, standardized weights are also important to have for comparing the relative influence of each of the feature variables. The difference between standardized and non-standardized coefficients illustrates the importance of being skilled in a variety of methods for interpreting and communicating machine learning results.

12.2 Multiple Linear Regression Diagnostics Checklist

We now review some of the key assumptions of multiple linear regression, applying it to the case study. We present the assumptions in the form of a model diagnostics checklist.

Linearity

In the chapter we noted that in MLR we assume that the relationship between each of the independent variables and the dependent variables is linear. The relationship can be measured in part by correlation. Although we started with *Income* as a feature, we eliminated it from our final model because it was not statistically significant and its correlation with the target variable *Income* was also weak. A correlation matrix displays the correlations among all the variables, as in Figure 12.3.

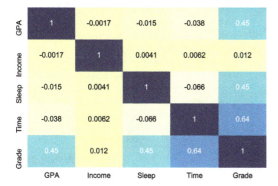

Figure 12.3: Correlations of the variables in the form of a heatmap.

For smaller datasets we can also review the correlations visually with a scatterplot. In Figure 12.4, the relationship between *Grade* and *Income* seems entirely random. It is confirmed by a very weak correlation of .01. Meanwhile, the correlation between *Grade* and *Time* spent studying seems to be the strongest.

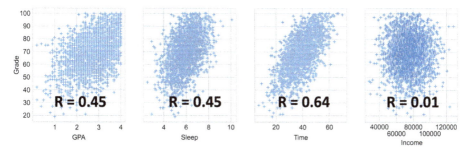

Figure 12.4: Scatterplots of the feature variables with the target variable, along with the correlations (R).

We add an important note of caution. A strong correlation between two variables doesn't necessarily mean that they are related linearly. Nor are we precluded from modeling non-linear phenomenon with linear models as long as we keep in mind that all models are approximations.

Normal Distribution of Error Terms

Our next assumption concerns the distribution of the error terms. Estimators of the model coefficients, along with confidence intervals, assume that the residuals follow a normal distribution. With smaller datasets, a *histogram* or *kde* distribution plot of the residuals provides the basis for a quick assessment.

Figure 12.5, for example, displays a histogram of the residuals from the multiple linear regression case study. The residuals seem to follow a normal distribution.

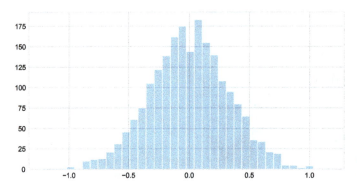

Figure 12.5: Histogram of residuals.

More generally, a *normal probability plot* or a *normal quantile plot* of the residuals is preferred. The plot shows the distribution of the percentiles against a theoretical normal distribution having the same mean and variance. If the distribution is normal, the points on such a plot should fall close to the diagonal reference line. Figure 12.6 displays a normal quantile plot of the residuals from the case study.

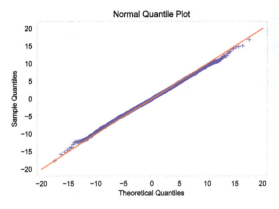

Figure 12.6: Normal Quantile Plot.

Finally, there are several statistical tests to check normality, including the *Kolomogorov-Smirnov* test, the *Shapiro-Wilk* test, the *Jarque-Bera* test, and the *Anderson-*

Darling test. The latter is considered among the best because it is specific to the normal distribution. Unlike many statistical tests, the *Anderson-Darling* test returns a list of critical values rather than a single *p-value*. Critical values provide a range of threshold levels for rejecting the *H0*, or the null hypothesis. The threshold level is called *alpha*, and is typically set at 5% (0.05).

In Python's SciPy implementation, one interprets *p-value* as follows:

- **p** ≤ *alpha*, retain H0, distribution is normal.
- **p** > *alpha*, reject H0, distribution is not normal.

The *Anderson-Darling* test statistic for the case study residuals is 0.243. Table 12.2 shows the critical values for several significance levels. Since the test static (0.243) is well below the critical values for all significance levels, the null hypothesis can be retained. The null hypothesis in this case states that the distribution of residuals is normal.

Table 12.2: Anderson-Darling test table of critical values and significance levels.

Critical Values	Significance Level
0.575	15
0.655	10
0.785	5
0.916	2.5
1.09	1

Multicollinearity

Multicollinearity is the occurrence of high intercorrelations among two or more independent variables in a multiple regression model. In our presentation of MLR in the concept chapter, we stated that the independent variables are truly indepedendent of one another. But that's in the ideal case. We can always expect *some* correlation among the independent variables. But there is a limit to the amount of correlation which can be tolerated by model estimators. Crossing the limit can lead to significant errors in the regression coefficient estimates.

There are a number of techniques for checking for multicollinearity that go beyond a simple inspection of a correlation matrix. A common method for detecting multicollinearity is by measuring *variance inflation factors* (VIF). Just like inflation in prices of products, multicollinearity inflates the estimates of the coefficients in a regression model. Hence the term "inflation" in VIF. A correlation matrix is limited in that it only probes for a bivariate relationship between independent variables, whereas VIF tests for correlation of a variable with a *group* of other variables.

Running a VIF test, available in the Python statsmodels library, on the case study feature variables results in the values shown in Table 12.3.

Table 12.3: Variance Inflation Factor.

Feature	VIF
GPA	1.0
Sleep	1.0
Time	1.0

A VIF number greater than 10 is considered high. We are below the threshold number and can proceed with the assumption that the feature variables are not plagued by multicollinearity.

Homoscedasticity

Homoscedasticity means that the variance of the residuals is nearly constant across the residual lines. Let's compare the two plots in Figure 12.7. Both represent plots of *Income* vs. *Consumption* in economics. In both cases, as *Income* increases, so does *Consumption*. The regression lines for both are very similar.

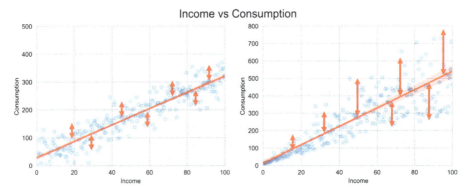

Figure 12.7: Income vs. Consumption for two different datasets.

But now let's compare the residuals of the two plots. In the left panel, the spread of the error terms is constant no matter where we look along the x-axis. By contrast, in the right panel the spread of the error term gets larger as x increases. What do we mean by the spread? It is the residual, or the distance of the actual point from the predicted point on the regression line. Homoscedasticity occurs when the spread remains constant throughout the *x*-axis. The violation of homoscedasticity is called heteroscedasticity. The error terms in the right plot are heteroscedastic. The spread increases as we move to the right in the graph.

An increase in the spread is only one of the ways in which heteroscedasticity can occur. We can envision a case where the spread is large in the beginning, gets smaller in the middle, and then gets large again. The key point is that in homoscedasticity the spread of error terms remains relatively constant throughout while in heteroscedasticity the spread of error terms varies. The contrast between homoscedasticity and heteroscedasticity is also shown in Figure 12.8, where we have a plot of the Income vs the Residuals.

Figure 12.8: The left panel is plot of the residuals. The right panel is a plot of the standardized residuals.

How might this occur with our example of *Income* vs. *Consumption*? The left and right panel in Figure 12.7 might express two different scenarios playing out in the real world. In the left panel, the behavior of *Income* vs. *Consumption* is captured adequately by a linear model. Indeed, as *Income* rises, so does *Consumption* in linear fashion. In the right panel, what might be occurring empirically is that as *Income* increases, while some consumers spend more, others spend less and increase their savings. The example illustrates the point that we have to look at the error terms to verify that we have met the assumptions of regression.

The assumption of homoscedasticity means that the variance of the error term or residual is the same (i. e. constant) across observations. No matter where we are on the *x*-axis, the spread of the errors should roughly be the same. For smaller datasets, we can inspect for homoscedasticity with visualizations. The left panel in Figure 12.9 shows fitted values versus residuals for the case study. The right panel plots fitted values versus standardized residuals. To spot homoscedasticity, there should be no visible pattern in the scatterplot (i. e., increase or decrease in the value of residuals).

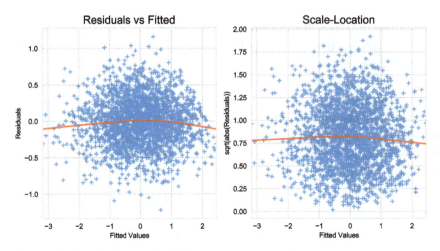

Figure 12.9: Detecting homoscedasticity.

The line should be more or less constant. From the plot, it appears that the model is homoscedastic.

For larger datasets, homoscedasticity is difficult to detect with visualizations. Fortunately, there are formal tests. Two common stastical tests are: *Breusch-Pagan* and *Goldfeld-Quandt*. When we run both on the case study model, we get the following results shown in Figure 12.10.

```
----Breusch-Pagan Test ----
                                value
Lagrange multiplier statistic     3.8
p-value                           0.3
f-value                           1.3
f p-value                         0.3


  ----Goldfeld-Quandt Test ----
             value
F statistic    1.0
p-value        0.3
```

Figure 12.10: Homoscedasticity statistical test results.

For both tests the null hypothesis assumes homoscedasticity. We *reject* the null hypothesis *only* if the *p-value* falls below a threshold value (e. g. 0.05). In both tests, the *p-value* is well above the threshold. Therefore, we can assume that the model is homoscedastic.

12.3 Summary

In this chapter, we introduced the topic of standardized coefficients. It is common in social science research journals to report the results of a multiple linear regression model in two columns. The first column reports unstandardized coefficients while the second column reports standardized coefficients. Standardized coefficients allow comparison of the influence of feature variables by putting everything into a common metric, namely standard deviation units. We then presented a diagnostics checklist for validating a number of critical assumptions behind multiple linear regression. These include checks for linearity, the normal distribution of error terms, multicollinearity, and homoscedasticity.

13 Multiple Linear Regression – Practice

The multiple linear regression case study tries to predict final exam *Grade* based on the feature variables *GPA*, *Sleep*, and *Time*. Earlier, we had eliminated *Income* from the list of feature variables. Our reasoning is given in the concept chapter for Multiple Linear Regression.

Import Python Libraries

We load the **pandas** library and the *ols* function from **statsmodels** library. The *ols* function is used to create the multiple regression model.

```
import pandas as pd
from statsmodels.formula.api import ols
```

Load and verify data

We load the 'academicperformance.csv' file into the dataframe *df* and check the first few records. The result is shown in Figure 13.1. *GPA* stands for grade point average. *Income* is family income in dollars. *Sleep* is the number of hours of sleep the student received the night before the exam. *Time* is the number of hours the student studied during the entire semester.

```
df = pd.read_csv("data/academicperformance.csv")
df.head()
```

	GPA	Income	Sleep	Time	Grade
0	2.9	82461	6.5	47	77
1	3.7	61113	6.2	47	94
2	2.8	63632	6.2	39	69
3	2.0	66854	7.2	49	81
4	2.8	82721	5.5	49	78

Figure 13.1: First few records of academic performance dataset.

Run Regression – statsmodels

We run multiple linear regression with *Grade* as the target variable and *GPA*, *Sleep*, and *Time* as the feature variables.

https://doi.org/10.1515/9781501505737-013

```
mlr = ols('Grade ~ GPA + Sleep + Time', df).fit()
```

Review results and model performance

The results of the regression are summarized in Figure 13.2. The intercept is [−39.7] and the coefficients are: [9.1, 7.2, 1.1]. The intercept and coefficients are all statistically significant. *R*-squared for the model is 0.89.

```
mlr.summary()
```

OLS Regression Results

Dep. Variable:	Grade	**R-squared:**	0.891
Model:	OLS	**Adj. R-squared:**	0.891
Method:	Least Squares	**F-statistic:**	5653.
Date:	Wed, 07 Jul 2021	**Prob (F-statistic):**	0.00
Time:	21:20:09	**Log-Likelihood:**	-6191.4
No. Observations:	2077	**AIC:**	1.239e+04
Df Residuals:	2073	**BIC:**	1.241e+04
Df Model:	3		
Covariance Type:	nonrobust		

	coef	std err	t	P>|t|	[0.025	0.975]
Intercept	-39.7098	0.879	-45.179	0.000	-41.434	-37.986
GPA	9.0992	0.136	67.065	0.000	8.833	9.365
Sleep	7.2070	0.104	69.500	0.000	7.004	7.410
Time	1.0580	0.011	95.102	0.000	1.036	1.080

Omnibus:	1.358	**Durbin-Watson:**	1.941
Prob(Omnibus):	0.507	**Jarque-Bera (JB):**	1.305
Skew:	-0.014	**Prob(JB):**	0.521
Kurtosis:	3.120	**Cond. No.**	344.

Figure 13.2: Summary report of regression.

Make predictions

We create a new data frame called *df_predict* to serve as input data to the model to generate predictions. The dataframe contains some combinations of *GPA*, *Sleep*, and *Time*. The predictions are shown in Figure 13.3.

The predictions are consistent with the coefficient estimates for the regression. A student who sleeps an additional hour, while holding *GPA* and *Time* constant should see an increase of 7.2 points (the coefficient for *Sleep*), which is what we see in the prediction in rows 0–2.

Each unit of increase in *GPA* corresponds to a 9.1 point increase in final *Grade*. This is shown in rows 3–5.

Finally, a student who practices 10 additional hours, while *GPA* and *Sleep* are held constant, should see a 10.6 point increase in their final *Grade*. This is shown in rows 6–8.

```
data = {'GPA':[3,3,3,2,3,4,2.5,2.5,2.5],
        'Sleep':[5,6,7,6,6,6,5,5,5],
        'Time':[30,30,30,30,30,30,40,50,60]}
df_predict = pd.DataFrame(data)
df_predict
```

	GPA	Sleep	Time	Grade
0	3.0	5	30	55.4
1	3.0	6	30	62.6
2	3.0	7	30	69.8
3	2.0	6	30	53.5
4	3.0	6	30	62.6
5	4.0	6	30	71.7
6	2.5	5	40	61.4
7	2.5	5	50	72.0
8	2.5	5	60	82.6

Figure 13.3: Prediction of new data.

14 Logistic Regression – Concept

In this chapter, we introduce logistic regression (LR) as one of the primary techniques for classification in supervised learning. Logistic regression is used primarily for binary classification, where the aim is to predict one of two possible outcomes. However, there are simple extensions for applying logistic regression to multinomial classification. Aside from being a powerful method for classification, our interest in logistic regression stems from its treatment of *probabilities*. An important theme of this chapter is how a formal understanding of probabilities can enhance decision and action.

> **Key Idea 1.** Logistic regression is a machine learning algorithm for predicting *binary outcomes*.
>
> **Key Idea 2.** LR allows multiple feature variables, both continuous and discrete. The target variable is a *probability* between 0 and 1.
>
> **Key Idea 3.** In LR, the output probability is converted to a binary outcome using a *threshold*. The default threshold is set at $p \geq .5$.
>
> **Key Idea 4.** The LR equation is expressed in two equivalent forms. In the first form, the output of the function is a probability. In the second form, the output of the function is the natural logarithm of the odds ratio. (We discuss this Key Idea more fully in the next chapter on theory.)

14.1 Bird's Eye View

In previous chapters, we saw that the goal of linear regression is to predict a continuous outcome. By contrast, in classification our goal is to predict categories or classes. A special case of classification is binary classification, where there are only two categories.

As in other cases of machine learning, we begin with a set of features X and try to predict an outcome y.

$$X \xrightarrow{\text{predicts}} y$$

In the case of logistic regression, y can only take on one or two possible values. What are some examples of binary classification?
- Will it snow tomorrow? (Figure 14.1).
- Is a credit card transaction fraudulent?
- Will Apple stock go up tomorrow?
- Is a tumor malignant?
- Will it rain tomorrow?

In each case, the question lends itself to a Yes/No answer.

Why use logistic regression? First, logistic regression is a natural extension of linear regression in terms of its structure. Second, logistic regression models probabili-

https://doi.org/10.1515/9781501505737-014

Will it snow tomorrow?

Yes

No

binary outcome **Figure 14.1:** Binary outcome yields a Yes/No answer.

ties. We model the outcome y indirectly through a probability p. The logistic regression function takes as input a feature vector X and outputs a probability p. If p is $\geq .5$, the output $y = 1$, otherwise $y = 0$. See Figure 14.2.

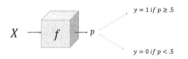

X —— f —— p

$y = 1\ if\ p \geq .5$

$y = 0\ if\ p < .5$

Figure 14.2: The output of logistic regression is a probability with a value between 0 and 1.

Why would we want to model probabilities? In machine learning, we want to predict the future. In the case of binary outcomes, we wish to know whether something will or will not occur. But very often, we want to know not just *that* something will occur but *how likely* is it to occur. And likelihood, of course, is captured by probabilities. Instead of predicting "yes" or "no," we can aim to predict probabilities as in Figure 14.3.

Will it snow tomorrow?

1

.3

0

probability

Figure 14.3: Whether it will snow tomorrow predicted as a probability.

14.2 Probabilities and Decision Making

How can this additional information about probabilities be helpful in decision making? First, we note a crucial fact about probabilities. A probability p is always between 0 to 1. If an outcome y has a probability of 1, it means that the outcome is certain. If the outcome y has probability of 0, it means that the outcome is impossible. But certainty and impossibility are the extremes. More likely is an outcome between 0 and 1. It is customary, though not required, to set the threshold for a binary outcome at $p \geq .5$. When a weather forecaster says it's "likely to rain tomorrow," she means that the probability is greater than .5. If she declares it is "very likely to rain tomorrow," the probability has inched its way upward nearer to 1. How might knowing the *exact probability* be useful?

As an example, let's consider the case of someone driving to work. Let's suppose that Mary normally drives to work each day. But when it snows, she prefers to take the train. Mary usually decides the night before whether to drive or to take the train. If the weather forecast of snow is probability of .7 or higher, Mary usually takes the train. If it is lower than .7, Mary drives to work. In this case, Mary set has her probability decision threshold at $p \geq .7$. See Figure 14.4.

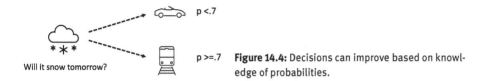

Will it snow tomorrow?

p <.7

p >=.7 **Figure 14.4:** Decisions can improve based on knowledge of probabilities.

Let's consider a more realistic example of decision and action based on probabilities. Let's suppose that a bank has developed and put in place a machine learning model for predicting loan defaults. Loan applications are scored and then fed to a machine learning model. Based on the model, loan applications are automatically accepted or rejected based on a default threshold of $p = .5$.

After a year, an internal study of the bank's loan policies arrives at some disturbing conclusions. First, the study suggests that some rejected loan applications ($p < .5$) were, in fact, a good risk and a loan should have been granted. Second, some granted loan applications ($p > .5$) were, in fact, bad risks and should not have been granted.

Based on the internal study and discussions with the community, the bank puts in place a new protocol. If for a loan application the probability of default is .3 or lower, the application is automatically approved. If the probability is .7 or greater, then the loan application is automatically rejected. Loan applications are automatically accepted or rejected at the two extremes. But loan applicants who fall in the middle (.3 to .7) are asked to provide additional data, which is then reviewed by a human examiner. If the loan is granted, a customer service agent is also required to provide additional follow-up services to ensure loan success. Using different thresholds to combine human and automated decision making is illustrated in Figure 14.5.

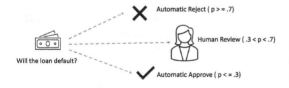

Will the loan default?

Automatic Reject (p > = .7)

Human Review (.3 < p < .7)

Automatic Approve (p < = .3)

Figure 14.5: Knowledge of probabilities also allows combining human and automated decision making.

One can imagine other examples where decision and action is improved by knowing not just *that* something might occur but *how likely* it is to occur. In many cases, there is a world of difference between a probability of .51 and .99, even though in a strictly binary sense both are in the same category.

Our example also shows how probabilities can be used to combine the power of machine and human intelligence.

14.3 Case Study: Credit Card Payments

Now that we have a basic understanding of logistic regression, let's deepen our understanding with a case study. For our case, we will develop a logistic regression model to predict credit card default.

Dataset

The dataset contains 10,000 records. A sample of observations is shown in Table 14.1. Our goal is to predict whether an individual is likely to default on their credit card payment. There are four variables in total: *default, student, balance,* and *income.* The variable *income* records the individual's annual income while *balance* is their monthly credit card balance. Both are continuous variables. The variable *student* is discrete (Yes or No) indicating student status. Finally, *default* is also discrete (Yes or No) indicating whether the individual was a student or not. (Note: *balance* and *income* are recorded in hundreds of dollars.)

Table 14.1: Loan Default Table.

default	student	balance	income
No	No	7.3	444
No	Yes	8.2	121
No	No	11	318
No	No	5.3	357
No	No	7.9	385

Exploratory Data Analysis

Basic summary statistics for *income* and *balance* are shown in Figure 14.6. Distributions of *income* and *balance*, in the form of a histogram, are shown in Figure 14.7.

The boxplots in Figure 14.8 displays of *balance* (left panel) and *income* (right panel) as a function of *default*. We can spot a noticeable difference in the two boxplots. *Balance* seems to play a far greater role in influencing *default* than does *income*.

	balance	income
count	10000.000000	10000.000000
mean	8.350900	335.174800
std	4.847527	133.363062
min	0.000000	8.000000
25%	5.000000	213.000000
50%	8.000000	345.500000
75%	12.000000	438.000000
max	27.000000	736.000000

Figure 14.6: Summary Statistics.

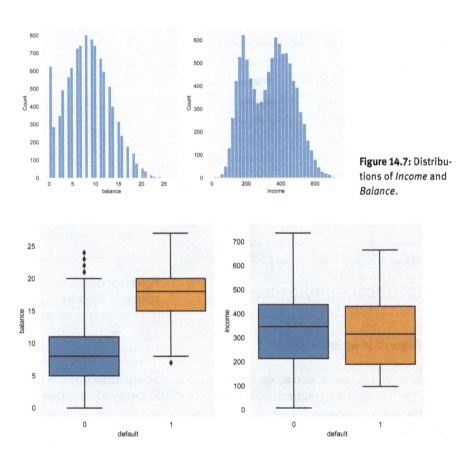

Figure 14.7: Distributions of *Income* and *Balance*.

Figure 14.8: Boxplots indicate that *balance* seems to influence *default* far more than *income*.

Logistic Regression with Income

We are now ready to run logistic regression. We select *default* as the target variable and *balance*, *income*, and *student* (status) as the feature variables.

$$default \sim balance + income + C(student)$$

A summary of the regression results is shown in Figure 14.9. We can see that *income* is not statistically significant. Its coefficient in the regression is also very low, indicating that it has a marginal effect on the target variable. Earlier, the boxplots also a revealed a very weak relationship.

Logit Regression Results

Dep. Variable:	default	No. Observations:	10000
Model:	Logit	Df Residuals:	9996
Method:	MLE	Df Model:	3
Date:	Wed, 30 Jun 2021	Pseudo R-squ.:	0.4614
Time:	09:11:22	Log-Likelihood:	-786.54
converged:	True	LL-Null:	-1460.3
Covariance Type:	nonrobust	LLR p-value:	7.010e-292

	coef	std err	z	P>|z|	[0.025	0.975]
Intercept	-10.8633	0.491	-22.107	0.000	-11.826	-9.900
C(student)[T.Yes]	-0.6449	0.236	-2.732	0.006	-1.107	-0.182
balance	0.5743	0.023	24.667	0.000	0.529	0.620
income	0.0002	0.001	0.296	0.767	-0.001	0.002

statistical significance

Figure 14.9: Logistic regression summary with *income*.

Logistic Regression without Income

Therefore, we run the regression again but this time leaving out *income* as a feature variable. The new results are summarized in Figure 14.10. We can see that this time, the coefficients and the intercept are statistically significant. Our final model, therefore, predicts loan default based on outstanding *balance* and *student* status.

Confusion Matrix

The accuracy score for the model is: .97. But as discussed in the chapters on model evaluation, accuracy score alone can be misleading in classification models. This is

Logit Regression Results

Dep. Variable:	default	No. Observations:	10000
Model:	Logit	Df Residuals:	9997
Method:	MLE	Df Model:	2
Date:	Wed, 30 Jun 2021	Pseudo R-squ.:	0.4614
Time:	09:11:28	Log-Likelihood:	-786.58
converged:	True	LL-Null:	-1460.3
Covariance Type:	nonrobust	LLR p-value:	2.499e-293

	coef	std err	z	P>|z|	[0.025	0.975]
Intercept	-10.7686	0.371	-29.019	0.000	-11.496	-10.041
C(student)[T.Yes]	-0.6993	0.147	-4.755	0.000	-0.988	-0.411
balance	0.5745	0.023	24.680	0.000	0.529	0.620

Figure 14.10: Logistic Regression summary with *balance* and student *status*.

especially the case when there is a category imbalance. In fact, in the dataset the imbalance is quite pronounced. The count of payment defaults is quite low compared to non defaults. See Table 14.2.

Table 14.2: Value counts for payment default.

default	count
No	9667
Yes	333

We are well advised, therefore, to generate a confusion matrix that generates matches and mismatches for both categories. A confusion matrix for the logistic regression model is shown in Figure 14.11. We can see right away that the model does quite well classifying the "No default" category, but its ability to predict "default" is weak.

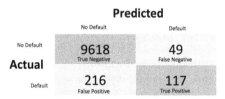

Figure 14.11: Confusion Matrix.

Classification Report

We can take model evaluation one step further by generating a classification report that displays Precision, Recall, and F1-score. The report is shown in Figure 14.12.

```
              precision    recall  f1-score   support

           0       0.98      0.99      0.99      9667
           1       0.70      0.35      0.47       333

    accuracy                           0.97     10000
   macro avg       0.84      0.67      0.73     10000
weighted avg       0.97      0.97      0.97     10000
```

Figure 14.12: Classification Report.

The Precision score for predicting defaults is .70. The Recall score is only .35. The F1-score is only .47.

Predictions

With the model, we are able to make predictions for new loan data. Table 14.3 shows probability predictions for several combinations of student *status* and *balance*.

Table 14.3: New Loan Predictions.

id	student	balance	probability	default
0	Yes	5.2	0.00	0
1	No	10.1	0.06	0
2	Yes	12.3	0.01	0
3	No	20.1	0.68	1
4	Yes	22.6	0.82	1

14.4 Summary

In this chapter, we introduced logistic regression as a major technique for binary classification. We illustrated how logistic regression yields classifications, but it does so through the intermediary of probabilities. We then showed how probabilities provide evidence for stronger decision-making, including combining machine intelligence with human intelligence. The case study for the chapter showed how different metrics can be applied in evaluating classification models. Given the relatively low recall score of the model in the case study, it is reasonable to conclude that the model is not strong enough yet to go into "production."

15 Logistic Regression – Theory

In this chapter, we continue our study of logistic regression. We begin by carefully examining the *structure* of the logistic regression equation. The form of the equation consists of two parts: a *linear* component and a *non-linear* component. Mathematically, logistic regression is an elegant instance of *function composition*, where two or more functions form an input-output chain. The concept of function composition will appear again in our study of deep learning. Next, we explain the concept of an *odds ratio*. Odds ratios play an important role in interpreting the coefficients of a logistic regression model.

> **Key Idea 1.** LR is based on a composition of two functions, written as $g(f(X))$. The first function f (the inner function) takes as input a set of features X and generates an output z. The second function g (the outer function) takes as input the output of the first function f and generates a probability p as output: $p = g(f(X))$.
>
> **Key Idea 2.** In LR, the first function f (the inner function) is the familiar function of multiple linear regression. The second function g (the outer function) is the *sigmoid function*.
>
> **Key Idea 3.** When used for binary classification, the output probability p is set to 1 or 0 based on a threshold. The default threshold is $p \geq .5$.
>
> **Key Idea 4.** In probability theory, odds (also called the odds ratio) is the probability of an event occurring divided by the probability of it not occurring: $o = \frac{p}{1-p}$
>
> **Key Idea 5.** The logistic regression equation can be expressed in two *equivalent forms*. In the first form, the output is a probability. In the second form, the output is the logarithm of the odds ratio.

15.1 Logistic Regression Function

In this section, we examine the structure of the logistic regression function. The structure consists of two parts, as shown in Figure 15.1. The first part is a linear function (f) which takes X, a vector of features, and outputs a continuous variable we call z. The second part is a non-linear function (g) which takes z as input and outputs a probability value p between 0 and 1.

Figure 15.1: Logistic regression function consists of two functions, f and g.

https://doi.org/10.1515/9781501505737-015

Linear component of logistic regression

Let's look now at the first function f in the chain. It's the familiar function from multiple linear regression. On the input side we have a vector X, which in the context of machine learning is a set of features. As we have seen, the linear regression function f transforms the input by applying a weight or coefficient $(\beta_1, \beta_2, \ldots, \beta_n)$ to each feature and then adding the intercept term (β_0).

The linear regression function is shown in Figure 15.2. We have labeled the output as z rather than y since it will be used as an input to the next function.

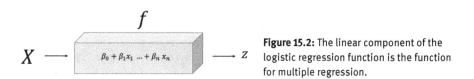

Figure 15.2: The linear component of the logistic regression function is the function for multiple regression.

Non-Linear component of logistic regression

Next, let's look at the second function g in the chain. The second function is called the *sigmoid* function, as shown in Figure 15.3.

$$g(z) = \frac{1}{1 + e^{-z}} = \frac{e^z}{e^z + 1}$$

The sigmoid function's domain is any real number from $[-\infty, +\infty]$. The function "squashes" the input so that the result is in the range $[0, 1]$. Figure 15.4 is a plot of the sigmoid function.

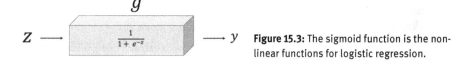

Figure 15.3: The sigmoid function is the non-linear functions for logistic regression.

Why is the sigmoid function used? Because its output yields a number in the range $[0, 1]$, which is the exact range of probabilities. While there are many functions which can perform this mathematical trick, the sigmoid function possesses a number of other properties vital to modeling probabilities correctly.

Now, we can express the logistic regression function as a chain, as shown in Figure 15.5.

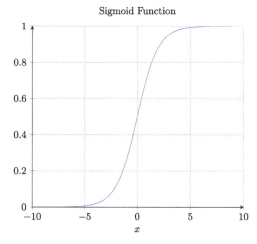

Sigmoid Function

Figure 15.4: The output of the sigmoid function ranges from 0 to 1, which is the same as the range for probabilities.

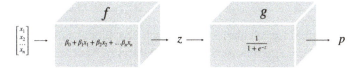

Figure 15.5: The logistic regression function can be viewed as a chain. The output of the first function f is fed as input to the second function g. The final output is a probability p.

Logistic regression equation step-by-step

Let's now examine the logistic regression equation step-by-step. The first function, the function of multiple regression, is expressed as:

$$f(X) = \beta_0 + \beta_1 x_1 + \beta_2 x_2 + \cdots \beta_n x_n \tag{15.1}$$

The second function, the sigmoid function, involves the constant e and is expressed as:

$$g(z) = \frac{1}{1 + e^{-z}} \tag{15.2}$$

The logistic function is a composition of the functions f and g. Function composition is written as $f(g(x))$, or, alternatively as $f \circ g$. We will use the former notation.

In Equation (15.1) we use z as the output of the multiple regression equation, which we then substitute in Equation (15.2) to get the first form of the logistic regression equation:

$$p = \frac{1}{1 + e^{-(\beta_0 + \beta_1 x_1 + \beta_2 x_2 + \cdots \beta_n x_n)}} \tag{15.3}$$

We note that the output of the logistic regression equation (Equation (15.3)) is a probability p.

15.2 Odds, Odds Ratio, and Logit

Now we come to a discussion of odds and odds ratios. Odds are merely a different way of speaking of probabilities, but it is crucial to interpreting logistic regression models.

The *odds* of an event is the ratio of the probability of an event occurring divided by it not occurring.

$$o = \frac{p}{1-p} \qquad (15.4)$$

Example 1: Coin Toss

Let's begin with some examples for calculating odds. The probability of a fair-sided coin landing as heads is $p = .5$. It also follows that the probability of it *not* landing as heads is $1 - p$, which is also .5.

In the case of the fair-sided coin landing as heads, the odds is 1:

$$\text{Odds(Heads)} = \frac{.5}{1 - .5} = 1$$

We note that the probability of a fair coin landing heads is .5, but the odds is 1.

Example 2: Dice Throw

Let's consider another example. The probability of rolling a 3 for a fair-sided dice is 1/6, or .17. The odds of rolling a 3 is:

$$\text{Odds(3)} = \frac{1/6}{5/6} = \frac{1}{5} = .2$$

Sometimes odds are also expressed as percentages. The odds of rolling a 3 is 20 %.

Odds and odds ratios are sometimes confused with one another. Odds expresses a ratio of probabilities. An odds ratio expresses a ratio of odds. Let's consider as an example gun ownership in the US. According to a US survey, about four-in-ten men (39 %) say they personally own a gun while the number is (22 %) for women. Let's work out the odds and odds ratios.

The probability that a man owns a gun in the US is .39. The probability that a woman owns a gun is considerably less at .22. From probabilities, we can calculate the odds of men and women owning guns:

$$\text{odds(men)} = \frac{.39}{.61} = .64$$

$$\text{odds(women)} = \frac{.22}{.78} = .28$$

The odds of gun ownership for men and women are .64 and .28, respectively.
Given the odds for both men and women, we can now calculate the odds ratio:

$$\frac{\text{odds(men)}}{\text{odds(women)}} = \frac{.64}{.28} = 2.28$$

The ratio of odds of men to women equals 2.28, which means that the odds of gun ownership is more than two times for men than for women. Odds ratios will prove useful when we need to interpret coefficients of a logistic regression model.

Thus far, we have discussed odds and odds ratios. But there is another step we need to be familiar with in order to understand the logistic regression equation fully. In the next section, we will see that the logistic regression equation can be expressed in two forms. The logit form of the equation has the output the logarithm of the odds, also called the logit L or logged odds.

$$L = \ln(o) = \ln\left(\frac{p}{1-p}\right)$$

Let's look at the logit transformation with two examples. If we begin with some probability, let's say $p = .2$, then $1 - p = .8$. The odds $o = \frac{.2}{.8} = .25$. The natural log or logit of .25 equals −1.39. If we begin with probability $p = .7$, then $1 - p = .3$. The odds $o = \frac{.7}{.3} = 2.33$. The logit of 2.33 equals 0.85.

We have seen how to go from probabilities to odds:

$$o = \frac{p}{1-p}$$

For the sake of completeness, we note that going from odds to a probability is just as easy:

$$p = \frac{o}{1+o}$$

If the odds is .25, then the probability $p = \frac{.25}{1.25} = .25$.

15.3 Logistic Regression Equation in Logit Form

Armed with the concept of odds, odds ratio and logit, we are now ready to express the formula for logistic regression in an alternative form.

Above, we stated the equation for logistic regression as:

$$\text{LR Equation:} \quad p = \frac{1}{1 + e^{-(\beta_0 + \beta_1 x_1 + \beta_2 x_2 + \cdots \beta_n x_n)}} \tag{15.5}$$

The benefit of this form of the equation is that it allows us to see that the output of the function is a probability p. When we run a logistic regression, it returns values for the intercept and the coefficients. But what do the values mean? How are they to be interpreted?

In order to attach a meaningful interpretation to the coefficients, we need to use an alternate formulation of the same equation. We will call the following alternative below the *logit form* of the equation.

$$\text{Logit Form:} \quad \ln\left(\frac{p}{1-p}\right) = \beta_0 + \beta_1 x_1 + \beta_2 x_2 + \cdots + \beta_n x_n \tag{15.6}$$

In the final section of this chapter, we show that the two forms are equivalent by formally deriving one from the other.

15.4 Interpreting the Coefficients

The *logit form* of the logistic regression equation allows us to interpret the results of a logistic regression in the same way we interpreted multiple regression.

Recall that in linear regression we interpreted the coefficients as follows: a unit change in an independent variables corresponds to an increase or decrease of one unit in the dependent variable multiplied by the corresponding coefficient. For example, in our case study for MLR one of the independent variables was *Sleep* (measured in hours) and the dependent variable was the final exam *Grade* (measured in points). The coefficient for *Sleep* was 7.21. We interpreted the result as: for each additional hour of Sleep, the exam *Grade* increases by 7.21 points.

In the case of logistic regression, the coefficients have exactly the same interpretation except that *units* of the dependent variable are log odds. Notice that the output in Equation (15.6) is the natural logarithm of the odds or the logit.

Let's apply this understanding to our case study. In the case study, the dependent variable was *default* on credit card payment. An independent variable was outstanding *balance* (in units of $100) on a loan. The logistic regression model yielded a coefficient of .57 for *balance*. We interpret this to mean that for each unit of increase in the *balance* increases the log odds of defaulting by .57. We can go from log odds to plain odds by exponentiating .57.

$$e^{.57} = 1.76$$

Thus, increasing the *balance* by $100 raises the odds by 1.76. This is equivalent to increasing the odds by .76 %.

15.5 Derivation of the Logistic Regression Equation as Log Odds

In this section we show that the two forms of the logistic regression equation are equivalent. The first form is useful for seeing that the output of logistic regression is a probability. The second form is useful in interpreting the coefficients of logistic regression as odds ratios.

We begin with the first formulation of the logistic regression equation:

$$P(z) = \frac{1}{1 + e^{-z}}$$

where,

$$z = \beta_0 + \beta_1 x_1 + \beta_2 x_2 + \cdots + \beta_n x_n$$

First, we rewrite the above more compactly as:

$$P = \frac{e^z}{1 + e^z}$$

$$1 - P = 1 - \frac{e^z}{1 + e^z}$$

Expressing the terms as a ratio:

$$\frac{P}{1 - P} = \frac{\frac{e^z}{1 + e^z}}{1 - \frac{e^z}{1 + e^z}}$$

$$\frac{P}{1 - P} = \frac{\frac{e^z}{1 + e^z}}{\frac{1 + e^z}{1 + e^z} - \frac{e^z}{1 + e^z}}$$

$$\frac{P}{1 - P} = \frac{\frac{e^z}{1 + e^z}}{\frac{1}{1 + e^z}}$$

$$\frac{P}{1 - P} = e^z$$

Taking the logarithm of both sides, we get:

$$\ln\left(\frac{P}{1 - P}\right) = z$$

Finally, substituting for Z we get:

$$\ln\left(\frac{P}{1-P}\right) = \beta_0 + \beta_1 x_1 + \beta_2 x_2 + \cdots + \beta_n x_n$$

15.6 Summary

We began the chapter by showing that the logistic regression function is an example of function composition. The function has two parts: a linear function and a non-linear function. The linear function takes a set of features as the input and returns the same result as that of multiple linear regression. The output of the linear function is then passed to the non-linear function as the input. The non-linear function is the sigmoid function, which squashes the input and produces an output in the range $[0, 1]$, which conforms to the range for probabilities. We then presented the concepts of odds and odds ratios as an alternative way of viewing probabilities. We concluded by demonstrating that the two forms of the logistic regression equation are equivalent.

16 Logistic Regression – Practice

The logistic regression case study tries to predict credit card *default* based on credit card *balance*, personal *income*, and student *status*.

Import Python libraries

We load the **pandas** and **numpy** libraries. We use **statsmodels** for the regression and metrics from **scikit-learn** library.

```python
import pandas as pd
import numpy as np

import statsmodels.api as sm
import statsmodels.formula.api as smf

from sklearn.metrics import confusion_matrix,
        classification_report, accuracy_score
```

Load and verify data

The credit card default data is loaded from a .csv file into a **pandas** dataframe. The first few records are shown in Figure 16.1.

```python
df = pd.read_csv('data/ccdefault.csv').round(1)
df.head()
```

	default	student	balance	income
0	No	No	729.5	44361.6
1	No	Yes	817.2	12106.1
2	No	No	1073.5	31767.1
3	No	No	529.3	35704.5
4	No	No	785.7	38463.5

Figure 16.1: First few records of credit card default dataset.

https://doi.org/10.1515/9781501505737-016

Clean data

The variables *default* and *student* are categorical variables. For machine learning, categorical variables need to be converted to numerical variables. In this case, we use **numpy** for making the conversion. However, a variety of techniques are available in Python.

We also transform the variables balance and income so that they are in units of 100s of dollars.

```
# remap default = 'Yes' to 1; 'No' to 0
df['default'] = np.where(df['default'] == "Yes", 1, 0)
df['student'] = np.where(df['student'] == "Yes", 1, 0)

# size balance and income to be 100s of $
df['balance'] = np.round(df['balance']/100,0)
df['income'] = np.round(df['income']/100,0)
```

Run Regression – statsmodels

We run the regression using **statsmodels**. The target variable is *default*. The feature variables are *balance* and *student*. In **statsmodels**, categorical variables are included in the formula as 'C(name of variable)'.

```
lr = smf.logit(formula='default ~ balance + C(student)',data=df).fit()
```

Review results and model performance

The regression summary report is displayed in Figure 16.2. Both variables are statistically significant. The coeffecients for *student* and *balance* are –0.7 and 0.57, respectively.

```
lr.summary()
```

Confusion Matrix

The confusion matrix is shown in Figure 16.3.

```
print(confusion_matrix(y,y_hat))
```

Logit Regression Results

Dep. Variable:	default	No. Observations:	10000
Model:	Logit	Df Residuals:	9997
Method:	MLE	Df Model:	2
Date:	Tue, 06 Jul 2021	Pseudo R-squ.:	0.4615
Time:	21:27:19	Log-Likelihood:	-786.44
converged:	True	LL-Null:	-1460.3
Covariance Type:	nonrobust	LLR p-value:	2.172e-293

	coef	std err	z	P>|z|	[0.025	0.975]
Intercept	-10.7703	0.371	-29.019	0.000	-11.498	-10.043
C(student)[T.1]	-0.7004	0.147	-4.761	0.000	-0.989	-0.412
balance	0.5746	0.023	24.680	0.000	0.529	0.620

Figure 16.2: Logistic Regression Summary Report.

```
[[9618    49]
 [ 216   117]]
```

Figure 16.3: Confusion Matrix of credit card default model.

Classification Report

The classification report is shown in Figure 16.4. Although accuracy is high at .97, the precision (.70) and recall scores (.35) are not impressive. The combined f1-score is only 0.47.

```
print(classification_report(y,y_hat))
```

```
              precision    recall  f1-score   support

           0       0.98      0.99      0.99      9667
           1       0.70      0.35      0.47       333

    accuracy                           0.97     10000
   macro avg       0.84      0.67      0.73     10000
weighted avg       0.97      0.97      0.97     10000
```

Figure 16.4: Classification Report of credit card default model.

Make predictions

We can predictions for new data using the *predict* method. It should be noted that for logistic regression, predictions are probabilities. The input for the predictions is the variable, *data_new*. The dataframe *df_new* is used to store the predictions. The predictions are shown in Figure 16.5.

```
# predict new points
data_new = {'balance': [5.2,10.1,12.3,20.1,22.6],
            'student': [1,0,1,0,1]}
df_new = pd.DataFrame(data_new)
df_new['probability'] = lr.predict(df_new).round(2)
df_new
```

	balance	student	probability
0	5.2	1	0.00
1	10.1	0	0.01
2	12.3	1	0.01
3	20.1	0	0.69
4	22.6	1	0.82

Figure 16.5: Probability predictions of new data.

17 *K*-Means – Concept

In this chapter, we turn to *unsupervised learning*. In supervised learning one or more features variables are used to predict a target variable. Given an input and an output, the goal in supervised learning is to discover a function that maps the input to the output. In unsupervised learning, there is no prediction. Nor is there any notion of error, since there is no output target to aim at. The goal in unsupervised machine learning is to discover interesting patterns or structures in the input data. Groups or clusters are one such hidden pattern. In this chapter we examine the *K*-Means algorithm, a widely used unsupervised learning technique for discovering hidden clusters in data.

> **Key Idea 1.** Unsupervised learning tries to discover hidden patterns or *structure* in data. Clusters are one such structure.
>
> **Key Idea 2.** The *K*-Means algorithm identifies *k* clusters in a dataset, where *k* is an integer specified beforehand.
>
> **Key Idea 3.** Each cluster in *K*-Means is defined by a single point called a *centroid*. A centroid is the mean of all the datapoints in the cluster.
>
> **Key Idea 4.** The *K*-Means algorithm uses a *distance metric* to identify the points belonging to each cluster.
>
> **Key Idea 5.** *K*-Means algorithm is iterative, meaning that it repeats a number of steps until it reaches a stop criterion.

17.1 Bird's Eye View

In unsupervised learning, our goal is discover hidden *structure* through data mining. We can think of the discovery process as similar to how a child learns to categorize the world. Initially, a child is confronted with a world of "blooming, buzzing confusion." From this initial chaos, the child learns to impose structure, including categories. Some categories are taught, while others are discovered by the child on its own.

In order to develop an intuitive understanding of *K*-Means, we begin with a before and after picture of categorization. For illustration, we use a simple two-dimensional dataset, as displayed in Figure 17.1. The before (left panel) is a set of uncategorized points. The after (right panel) is the same set categorized into two clusters.

In our trivial example, it's simple to discern the two clusters visually. But in the world of Big Data, we seldom have recourse to discovering structure by means of simple inspection. The number of points, the dimensions of the dataset, and the number of clusters can all be quite large. Hence the need for an algorithm such as *K*-Means.

https://doi.org/10.1515/9781501505737-017

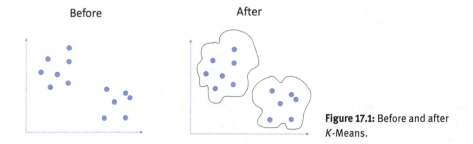

Figure 17.1: Before and after *K*-Means.

K-Means is an elegant technique for partitioning a dataset into *k* non-overlapping clusters. The instructions to *K*-Means are: "Here is a dataset. Find *k* clusters in the dataset." At this point, the algorithm takes over.

Let's look at how *K*-Means works.

K-Means Algorithm Steps.

- **Step 0:** Set a value for *k*, the number of clusters. The value is set beforehand.
- **Step 1:** From the dataset the *K*-Means algorithm randomly selects *k* points, which serve as the initial centers or *centroids* of the *k* clusters.
- **Step 2:** The algorithm assigns each point in the dataset to the *closest* centroid, thus forming *k* groups.
- **Step 3:** The algorithm then computes *new centroids* by calculating the *mean* of each group.
- **Step 4:** The algorithm repeats Steps 2 and 3 until it reaches a stop criterion.

Let's go through each step as shown in Figures 17.2 and 17.3.

In Step 0, we have a set of data points. We have also decided to use *k* = 2 as the number of clusters we want the algorithm to find in the dataset.

In Step 1, the algorithm *randomly* chooses two points C1 and C2 as the two centers for the clusters. The two points are randomly chosen typically from the existing data points.

Figure 17.2: Steps 0 to 2.

In Step 2, the algorithm calculates the distance of each point to the two centroids. It assigns each point to the closest centroid.

Step 3

Step 4

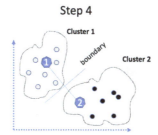

Figure 17.3:
Steps 3 and 4.

In Step 3, the algorithm calculates the *means* of the two clusters, which then become the new centroids.

In Step 4, each point is reassigned to Cluster 1 or Cluster 2 based on their proximity to the new centers. The process is repeated until there are no new assignments and we converge towards a stable set of clusters.

17.2 Case Study: Marketing Segmentation

Now that we have an overview of K-Means clustering, let's put it in action with a case study in marketing segmentation. Our case involves data collected from shoppers at a retail mall. Using clustering we would like to determine if there is an interesting pattern among shoppers that we can leverage for the marketing team.

The dataset consists of *Gender, Age, Income,* and shopping *Score. Income* is the shopper's yearly income. Shopping *Score* is an index of the customer's purchases at the mall. A higher index means that the customer purchases more goods and services relative to other customers. Table 17.1 displays sample records from the dataset.

Table 17.1: Mall Customer Data.

ID	Gender	Age	Income	Score
0	Male	19	15	39
1	Male	21	15	81
2	Female	20	16	60
3	Female	23	16	77
4	Female	31	17	40

A starting question, of course, is: How many clusters are there in the dataset? Unfortunately, there is no right answer. The K-Means algorithm will look for whatever number of clusters (k) is provided beforehand. In the next chapter, we will develop some heuristics for choosing a value for k. For this exercise, we will guess, based on domain knowledge, that there are likely to be five types of shoppers. Accordingly, we will set the value as $k = 5$.

We go ahead and run the *K*-Means algorithm against the dataset. It returns by categorizing each point into one of five clusters. The categorization is shown in Figure 17.4. The algorithm doesn't tell us, however, what meaning to attach to the groups. In other words, *K*-Means does not return semantic information with the clusters.

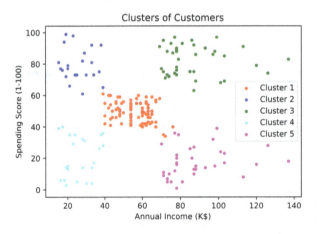

Figure 17.4: Running *K*-Means with *k* = 5 reveals 5 clusters. The algorithm does not tell us how the clusters should be interpreted.

Attaching a *meaning* to the clusters is the most important step in using clustering. It also requires a high level of domain knowledge that most data scientists lack. Therefore, we can imagine that the company sets up a collaborative meeting between the data science and business teams. The goal of the meeting is to determine whether the discovered clusters correspond to anything real.

After much debate, the business and technical teams come up with a provisional interpretation for the clusters. The team suggests the following interpretation:

– **Middle-of-the-road**: *moderate income, moderate spend*. The middle-of-the-road group has moderate income and spends a moderate amount for goods and services at the mall.
– **Browser**: *low income, low spend*. The browser group lacks disposable income and comes to the mall mostly to browse.
– **Conservative**: *high income, low spend*. The conservative group has considerable disposable income but tends not to spend very much at this particular mall.
– **Enthusiastic**: *low income, high spend*. The enthusiastic group has low income but tends to spend high amounts.
– **Luxury**: *high spend, high income*. The luxury group has high income and also spends high amounts.

Based on the grouping, the marketing team sets a provisional strategy. The starting point of the strategy is the observation that it is always cheaper to retain customers than to acquire new ones. The first aspect of the strategy is to encourage greater loyalty among the high-spend groups. Both clusters (luxury and enthusiastic) have a high spend.

The retention strategy for both is to provide enhanced services. The business unit's hypothesis is that *enthusiastic* shoppers come to the mall mostly to find good bargains. Enhanced service for the group will consist of better communication on upcoming bargains and additional discounts at the time of purchase.

The hypothesis about the *luxury* group is they come to the mall mostly to shop at a couple of the high-end stores and restaurants. For them, a concierge service is proposed, including free valet parking. It is agreed at the meeting that additional data needs to be collected to confirm the hypotheses about the two groups. A follow-up meeting will investigate the hypotheses in more detail.

17.3 Summary

In this chapter, we examined the K-Means algorithm as a form of unsupervised learning. In unsupervised learning, there is no output. We only have input data and the aim is to discover hidden structure, such as groups or clusters. The K-Means algorithm discovers hidden groups in a dataset, but the number of groups (k) must be specified beforehand. We saw how K-Means can be used for customer segmentation. Once the groups are identified, a company can set different strategies for different groups. K-Means, therefore, can be a powerful tool for customer segmentation. But clustering is not restricted to customer relationship management. It is being used widely in an array of applications, ranging from bioinformatics to speech recognition.

18 *K*-Means – Theory

In the previous chapter, we saw that the *K*-Means algorithm partitions a dataset into a pre-specified number of groups or clusters. *K*-Means is at once simple and powerful. Using a few lines of code, it is possible to discover patterns beyond the ken of human insight. But *K*-Means, along with all machine algorithms, is based on assumptions. These assumptions impose important limits on discovery and how results should be interpreted. In this chapter, we review some assumptions about *K*-Means and discuss their implications for model interpretation. We also provide some heuristics for selecting an initial *k*.

Key Idea 1. The *K*-Means algorithm is based on a family of iterative algorithms called Expectation – Maximization.

Key Idea 2. In *K*-Means, the choice of initial centroids can affect the discovery of clusters.

Key Idea 3. In *K*-Means, clusters are partitioned using linear boundaries. This can make *K*-Means ineffective for recognizing complex geometries.

Key Idea 4. In *K*-Means, the value of *k* is chosen beforehand. A number of heuristics are available to select an *optimal k*.

18.1 Expectation – Maximization

Let's review our understanding of *K*-Means with a simple example. Consider a dataset that contains 4,000 of the largest cities of the world along with their latitude and longitude. The first few rows of the dataset is shown in Table 18.1.

Table 18.1: World cities with their longitude and latitude.

City	Longitude	Latitude
Livingstone	25.85425	−17.84194
Kitwe	28.21323	−12.80243
Chingola	27.88382	−12.52897
Harare	31.05337	−17.82772
Epworth	31.14750	−17.89000

If we give *K*-Means the value of $k = 6$, the algorithm quickly discovers the pattern we immediately recognize as the major populated continents. The result is shown in Figure 18.1. The classification matches North America, South America, Africa, and Europe fairly well. Asia, however, is divided into two regions, with Australia falling within one of the two. *K*-Means' discovery is impressive, since it is based only on two items of information: latitude and longitude.

https://doi.org/10.1515/9781501505737-018

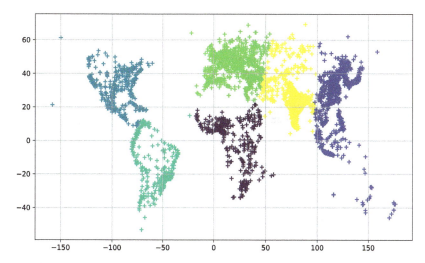

Figure 18.1: The world's largest cities as clustered by K-Means algorithm.

How was the clustering accomplished? In the previous chapter, we saw that K-Means is based on two basic ideas:

- The centroid or cluster center is the mean of all the points in the cluster.
- Each point in the cluster is closest to its centroid compared to other centroids.

The algorithm behind K-Means is based on a powerful family of algorithms called Expectation – Maximization (EM). In the case of K-Means, EM proceeds as follows:

Expectation – Maximation.
- Guess the *initial values* for the centroids
- **Expectation Step**: Assign each point to the nearest centroid.
- **Maximization Step**: Reset the cluster centers to the mean of each cluster.
- Repeat **EM** until convergence is reached.

The Expectation Step is called 'expectation' because during each cycle we update our expectation of where the centers are located. The Maximization Step is called 'maximization' because the algorithm is based on a function which maximizes the probability of pinning down the "correct" centers. In the case of K-Means, we do so by taking the mean of the data points in each cluster. Figure 18.2 displays a flow chart of the Expectation-Maximization algorithm.

Initial choice of centroids

Let's look now at some of the consequences of the algorithm's assumptions. One consequence is that the initial choice of centroids matters. By default, K-Means chooses

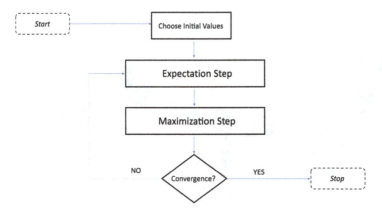

Figure 18.2: Expectation – Maximization Algorithm.

the initial set of centroids randomly, which means that different choices can some-times lead to different results. For example, the dataset of cities leads to a different set of clusters at different times. Sometimes, the end result can be poor or misleading. Figure 18.3 shows that this time Africa and Europe are placed in the same cluster and Asia is broken up into three separate clusters. Although this grouping might not be poor, it does illustrate that *K*-Means does not guarantee a single "correct" result.

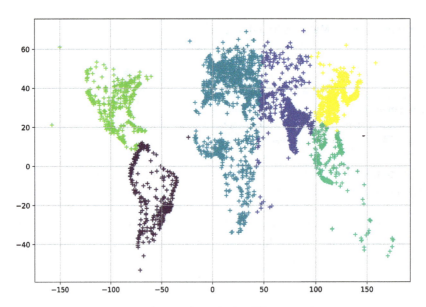

Figure 18.3: The initial choice of centroids can lead to different results.

Why does this matter? Imagine that we apply K-Means in criminology, an area with obvious ethical implications. But how people end up being grouped is the result of an automated algorithm with different results at different times. The different results are also not easily explained. From an ethical point of view, this state of affairs is obviously problematic.

Some of these quirks are unavoidable, given the nature of the algorithm. However, most implementations come with helpful hyperparameters. For example, in *scikit-lrn*'s implementation of K-Means, the default method for initialization of centroids is 'k-means++' (rather than 'random'), which means that the initial cluster centers are chosen in a "smart" way.

What does this entail? It means that *scikit-lrn* runs the algorithm 10 times with different random initializations. It returns the best result from the 10, where best means that the sum of variances of the clusters is the smallest. A smarter choice also speeds up convergence. In the world cities example, it takes approximately 16 iterations for convergence with a random choice compared to only 6 with a smart choice. The contrast might seem trivial, but for large, complex datasets a smart choice for initial centroids can speed up computation enormously and lead to better results.

Linear decision boundaries

The fundamental assumption of K-Means is that each point is closer to its cluster center than to any others. The consequence is that K-Means is often ineffective for complex geometries.

Figure 18.4 shows three clusters and *linear decision boundaries*, which is a consequence of K-Means. But this severely limits the types of clusters that can be discovered by K-Means.

Consider now the set of points in Figure 18.5. The two clusters discovered by K-Means are based on drawing linear boundaries. Therefore, it unable to recognize the two half moons as distinct clusters.

Fortunately, there are techniques such as spectral clustering and Gaussian Mixture Models that extend the capabilities of K-Means to discern complex geometries. When we apply spectral clustering, as shown in Figure 18.6, we get the expected two half moons.

18.2 Choice of K

We have noted that K-Means itself does not choose k. It is specified beforehand for the algorithm to work. Is there a way of choosing the "optimal" number of clusters? While there is no single correct answer, there are a couple of techniques we can use for

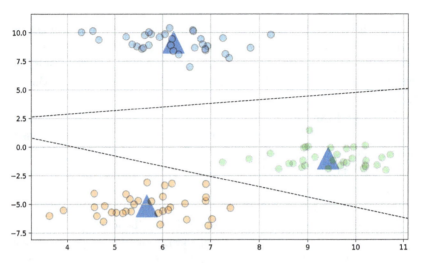

Figure 18.4: *K*-Means separates clusters using linear boundaries.

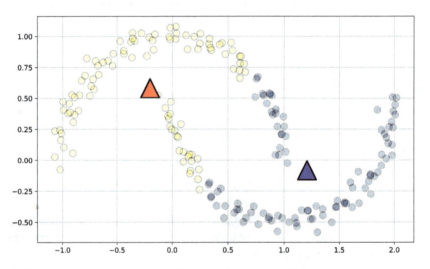

Figure 18.5: *K*-Means does a poor job distinguishing clusters with complex geometries.

guidance. The first is called *inertia* (also known as the *elbow method*), and the second is called *silhouette*.

Let's look again at the mall customer dataset used in the previous chapter. Using *K*-Means, we clustered the data into five groups or $k = 5$. The clusters are shown in Figure 18.7.

In looking at clusters, we can distiguish between two types of distances: intercluster and intracluster. "Intra" means distances between points within or inside a cluster. "Inter" means distances between clusters. Inertia measures intracluster distance. It

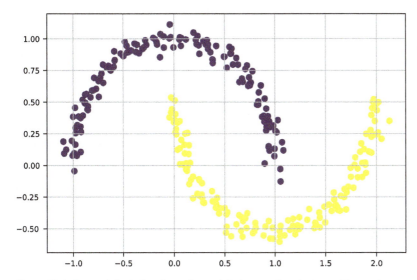

Figure 18.6: Spectral clustering does a better job demarcating clusters with complex geometries.

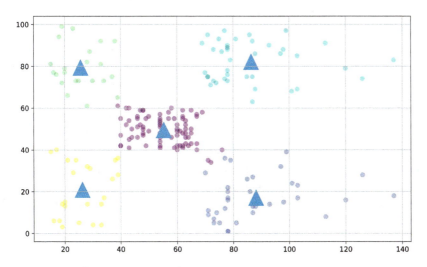

Figure 18.7: Mall customers clustered with K-Means.

calculates the sum of the squared distances of each point to its center. In concept, it is similar to mean squared error. The smaller the inertia, the more compact the clusters. Figure 18.8 shows a plot of k vs. *inertia* for the mall customer data.

According to the inertia or elbow method, the optimal size for k is at the elbow point. The values for k begin to decline, and at the "elbow" the descent is linear with a very slope. In our case of the mall customers, the ideal k is 5.

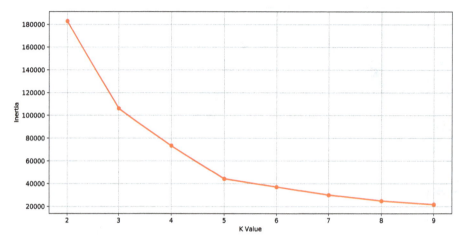

Figure 18.8: Inertia or Elbow Method.

Inertia measures the cohesion of points within a cluster. It tells us that points within a cluster are closely bound together. However, it tells us very little about cluster separation. A variety of techniques incorporate intercluster distance for determining the optimal value for k in K-Means. Intercluster distance measures the separation between clusters. Ideally, clusters should be both compact and far apart. Metrics such as Dunn Index and Silhouette consider both intracluster and intercluster distance. The silhouette metric, for example, is a ratio. The measure has a range of $[-1, 1]$. A value near +1 indicates that a point is close to the set of points in its own cluster and far from points in other clusters, which is the balance we want. The best value is 1 and the worst value is –1. Values near 0 indicate overlapping clusters.

Figure 18.9 shows the silhouette scores for various k for the customer mall data. As in the case of inertia, a value of $k = 5$ seems to be optimal. We conclude by emphasizing once again that these techniques for finding the optimal are, at best, heuristics. The ultimate judgment will always be pragmatic in nature.

18.3 Summary

In this chapter, we began by noting that K-Means belongs to a family of algorithms based on Expectation – Maximization. We then highlighted a couple of consequences of the algorithm. The first concerns the initial choice of centroids. The second concerns the linear nature of the boundaries used for partitioning. Both can result in unexpected or undesirable results. We then considered a couple of techniques for determining an "optimal" value for choosing k. But we added the caution that such choices require human judgment and should not be left entirely to machines.

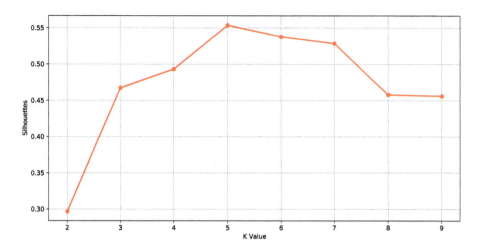

Figure 18.9: *k* Values vs, Silhouette Score.

19 *K*-Means – Practice

For the case study, we try to discover meaningful customer groups for market segmentation.

Import Python libraries

First, we load **pandas, matplotlib, seaborn**, and *KMeans* module from the **scikit-learn** library.

```python
import pandas as pd
from sklearn.cluster import KMeans

import matplotlib.pyplot as plt
import seaborn as sns
```


Load and verify data

Next, we load and verify the data. Although there are four columns, we only use *Income* and *Score* for clustering. *Income* is the customer's personal income. *Score* is an indexed score of how much the customer spends at the mall.

```python
df = pd.read_csv("data/mallcustomers.csv")
df.head()
```


Run *K*-Means

Next, we run *K*-Means with k (number of clusters) set at $k = 5$.

```python
X = df[['Score','Income']]
km = KMeans(n_clusters=5).fit(X)
```


Prepare dataframe for displaying results

We can retrieve the results of the clustering by using the *predict* method. We create a dataframe (*df_c*) to represent the categorizations.

https://doi.org/10.1515/9781501505737-019

```
results = km.predict(X)
clusters = pd.DataFrame(results,columns=['cluster'])

df_c = X.join(clusters, how='outer')
df_c.head()

category = {0:'Enthusiastic', 1:'Conservative',
            2:'Middle-of-the-Road', 3:'Browsers',4:'Luxury'}

df_c['cat'] = df_c['cluster']
df_c = df_c.replace({'cat':category})
```

Display results

We display the results of the categorization with a **seaborn** scatterplot, as shown in Figure 19.1.

```
plt.figure(figsize=(12,6))
sns.scatterplot(x="Income",y="Score",data=df_c,hue="cat",
                palette="deep",size="Score")
```

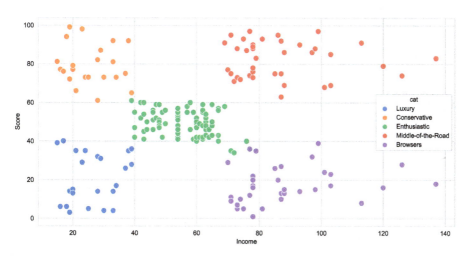

Figure 19.1: Mall Customers Clusters.

Part IV: **Deep Learning**

20 Deep Learning – Bird's Eye View

We are now ready to begin our study of deep learning. The variety of deep learning networks can be understood in terms of a modest set of foundational principles. In this chapter, we state five principles which lie at the core of artificial neural networks. We then synthesize the foundational principles by using the analogy of a law court. Deep learning networks are based on hierarchical representation of data. We compare the formation of this hierarchical representation to the process of reaching judgment in a law court.

20.1 Foundational Principles

Principle 1. A *neuron* is the atomic computational unit of a deep learning network.

Neurons are the atomic building blocks of deep learning networks. Each neuron performs a simple two-step computation. During the first step, the neuron takes in one or more inputs, multiplies each input by a weight, sums the weighted input values, and adds a bias term. During the second step, the output of the first computation is sent as input for a second computation.

Principle 2. Neurons are organized in a set of connected *layers*.

Just as atoms combine to form molecules, neurons combine to form layers. Neurons are organized in vertical stacks called layers. Neural networks have three types of layers. The input layer consists of input data only. There are no neurons in the input layer. Next, there is a series of one or more hidden layers. Finally, the output layer consists of one or more neurons which produce the final output.

Principle 3. *Forward propagation* through the layers is the computational process for generating predictions.

In a neural network, the process of generating predictions begins with input data being sent to the first layer. The layer computes an output and sends the result to the next layer. The process of "forward propagation" continues until the final layer is reached. The neurons in the final layer compute the output.

During the process of forward propagation, data begins with raw input. As it moves through the series of layers, it is incrementally transformed into more abstract representations. For example, in image recognition, the starting input is a set of pixels. As the data moves through the first layers, neurons combine the pixels to recognize strokes and edges of different orientations. As the data moves further, later layers recognize more complex structures such as lines, arcs, and corners. These are

https://doi.org/10.1515/9781501505737-020

then combined further to represent circles, squares, and so on. As the final layers are reached, the network is able to represent final shapes such as faces.

Principle 4. A *loss function* measures the error by comparing the prediction against the true value.

Forward propagation takes raw input and performs a series of data transformations to produce a final output. At the beginning stages, the neural network has not "learned" the proper settings to produce an accurate output. At the end of each forward propagation step, a loss function compares the output or prediction to the true value (what the network should output). Estimating the error is a crucial prelude to adjusting the network settings to produce more accurate predictions. The loss function computes a distance score that captures how well the network has done in producing the expected output.

Principle 5. *Backward propagation* is the learning process by which the network adjusts its parameters.

Backward propagation is the central algorithm in deep learning. The network's output is based on the initial settings of the neurons. We can think of each neuron as consisting of a set of gears. The gear settings determine the output. The loss function provides a signal to the backpropagation algorithm, which uses the error estimate to adjust the individual "parameters" (gear settings) of every neuron. The reason why it's called backward propagation is because the process of adjusting the network parameters proceeds in reverse. The backpropagation algorithm adjusts the neurons in the last layer first, and then proceeds sequentially through the hidden layers until it reaches the first layer.

20.2 From Evidence to Judgment

To build our intuition of how artificial neural networks work, we use the analogy of a law court. Let's imagine a law court in which a judgment has to be rendered. Our law court is simplified, so it has only three actors: witnesses, a deliberative body, and judges. In deep learning, the witnesses correspond to the input layer. The deliberative body corresponds to the hidden layers. The judges correspond to the output layer. The witnesses provide the data, testimony, or evidence. The deliberative body weighs and synthesizes the evidence of the witnesses. The judges act as arbiters and issue the final case ruling. The three aspects of deep learning are shown in Figure 20.1.

This characterization of deep learning as a court of law is a first approximation. To round out the picture, we need to introduce two other key ideas. The first idea is that the deliberative body is not a single entity but several groups connected to each other in a chain. We will see later that each deliberative group corresponds to a "layer" of

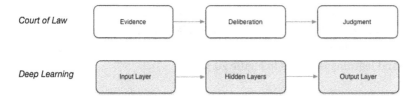

Figure 20.1: Deep Learning can be viewed as a Law Court with three main actors.

the neural network. The first group weighs the evidence from the witnesses, passing its work to the second group. The second group synthesizes the work of the first group, transmitting it in turn to the third group. This sequence continues until the chain of information reaches the judges for a final ruling. In general, each group or layer in the sequence synthesizes information from the previous group, adding its own expertise, before passing on its evaluation to the next group in the chain. Each group in the chain is also able to form concepts and make judgments at a higher level of abstraction than its predecessor group. This sequencing of deliberation in groups accounts for the *hierarchical nature* of deep learning. The flow of information from initial evidence to final judgment is called forward propagation. The chain of deliberation is shown in Figure 20.2.

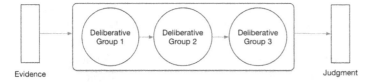

Figure 20.2: Deliberation is the process of taking in evidence and reaching a judgment. The process occurs in stages with several deliberative groups.

The second key idea is that the deliberative body and judges are initially inexperienced. They appear on the scene as novices and have to be trained in the law before they are assigned cases. Just as law students acquire expertise in the law by studying and applying historical cases, a neural network is "trained" with a large set of historical examples. The "court-in-training" is given training examples (i. e. witnesses and their testimony) unaware of the correct historical ruling. The court-in-training issues a "hypothetical" ruling, which serves as a form of practice. The hypothetical ruling is then compared with the correct ruling. The comparison evaluates whether the hypothetical ruling is correct, but also measures the size of the error or discrepancy. In deep learning the error between the correct result and the hypothetical result is captured formally by a loss function. Once the discrepancy is understood, feedback is provided to every member in the chain. Each member in the adjusts the "weight" they give to each witness or piece of evidence. This learning of the law takes place through multiple cycles of error, feedback, and correction in the weights and biases used to evaluate the evidence. This cycle of learning is called backward propagation. The cycle of measuring error and learning is shown in Figure 20.3.

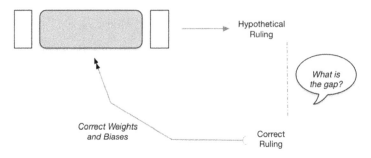

Figure 20.3: The learning process involves measuring error and updating weights and biases.

20.3 Summary

The process of learning in a neural network is summarized in Deep Learning Big Picture, Figure 20.4. The basic computational unit of a neural network is a neuron. A neuron computes its output based on its weights, which can be thought of as gears in a machine. Neurons are organized in computational layers that take an input X and produce a prediction $\hat{y}$. The computation takes place through the succession of layers. A neural network can contain millions of individual neurons, but for our purposes it can be thought of as a single function that computes an output based on an input. Once the prediction is computed, a *loss function* compares the prediction ($\hat{y}$) against the true target (y) to compute the error. The error is the loss score. At the next stage of backward propagation, an optimizer uses the loss score as a signal to adjust or update the neuron's weights and biases. The role of the optimizer is to calculate how much

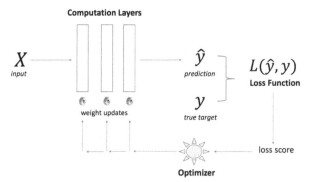

Figure 20.4: Deep Learning Big Picture.

or how little each neuron's weights and biases have to be changed to bring the prediction in alignment with the ground truth. The cycle of forward propagation, error check, and backward propagation continues repeatedly until the network reaches an acceptable level of loss.

21 Neurons

The neuron is the basic building block of an artificial neural network. A neuron has one and only purpose in life: it is to perform a simple two-step computation. In this chapter, we describe this computation in detail.

> **Key Idea 1.** A neuron computes a single number.
>
> **Key Idea 2.** A neuron computes its output in two steps. The first computation is *linear*. The output of the first computation is fed as an input to the second computation. The second computation is *non-linear*.
>
> **Key Idea 3.** The first step of neural computation is performed by the *transfer function*. The transfer function is the same in all neurons. The second step is performed by an *activation function*. The activation function in a neuron varies, depending on the deep learning task.
>
> **Key Idea 4.** The most common activation functions in deep learning are the *ReLU* and *sigmoid* functions.

21.1 Neurons as Functions

A biological neuron (Figure 21.1) receives input signals through its dendrites. It processes the signals in the body or soma. It then transmits the computed signal to other neurons through synapses.

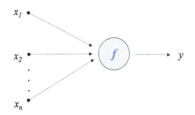

Figure 21.1: Biological Neuron. Wikicommons. License under Creative Commons CC0.

An artificial neuron has a similar structure. It receives input signals through its inbound connections from other neurons, performs a computation on the input signals, and then passes its output to other neurons. An artificial neuron is expressed as a mathematical function. It receives a set of inputs $x_1, x_2 \ldots, x_n$, performs a computation on the inputs, and produces an output y, as shown in Figure 21.2.

Figure 21.2: A neuron is a function which takes multiple inputs and computes an output.

https://doi.org/10.1515/9781501505737-021

A neuron computes its output in two steps, as shown in Figure 21.3. The first step is a *linear* function, which we write as $f^{(1)}$. The first function operates on the incoming input using only addition and multiplication. The output of the first function is then passed on to a second function, which we write as $f^{(2)}$. The second function is *non-linear*. The result of the second function's computation is the output of the neuron.

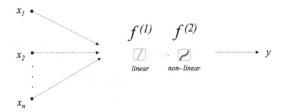

Figure 21.3: Neurons perform their computation in two steps. Each step is performed by a different function.

This idea of chaining, where the output of one function is fed as an input to a second function, is called *function composition* in mathematics. The linear function in neural networks is called the *transfer function*. We represent the transfer function equivalently as $f^{(1)}$ and Σ. The non-linear function is called the *activation function*. We represent the activation function equivalently as $f^{(2)}$ and ϕ.

Figure 21.4 shows neural computation as function composition. When expressed as function composition, the order of execution is from right to left. The "inner function" $f^{(1)}$ is computed first, its output is then fed as an input to the "outer function" $f^{(2)}$.

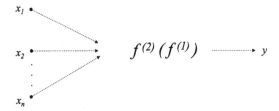

Figure 21.4: A neuron's computation can be represented as function composition.

Neural computation: Step 1

Let's look at Step 1 of the computation with an example. Imagine a situation in which we have to make a decision, such as buying a car. During deliberation, we might consult a variety of individuals, including car experts and casual strangers. In arriving at a decision, we attach different weights to different individuals. In the same way, a neuron attaches different *weights* to different inputs.

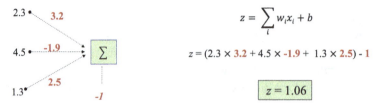

Figure 21.5: Computation Example, Step 1.

The neuron in Figure 21.5 has three inputs: $x_1 = 2.3$, $x_2 = 4.5$, and $x_3 = 1.3$. The neuron associates a weight to each input: $w_1 = 3.2$, $w_2 = -1.9$, and $w_3 = 2.5$. It also attaches a bias term $b = -1$. For the moment, we will ignore where the values of the weights and biases come from, except to note that the values *change* during the process of learning.

The computation during the first step is simply the *weighted sum* of the inputs plus the bias. The output of the computation in the first step is stored in the intermediate variable z.

For our example, the value of z is calculated as:

$$z = (2.3 \times 3.2) + (4.5 \times -1.9) + (1.3 \times 2.5) - 1 = 1.06$$

In general, if there are n inputs to the neuron, then the formula for computation in the first step is:

$$z = x_1 w_1 + x_2 w_2 + \cdots + x_n w_n + b$$

Using the summation convention, we can express the formula for neural computation in the first step as:

$$z = \sum_{i=1}^{n} w_i x_i + b \qquad (21.1)$$

The formula for computation in this first step should be familiar. It is the formula for multiple regression, except we have used w_i to express the coefficients and b to express the intercept. A single neuron can perform multiple regression!

Neural computation: Step 2

Let's now examine Step 2 of the computation. The first step of the computation yielded the output z. In Step 2, z is fed as an input to a second function.

Deep learning networks use a variety of non-linear functions during the second stage of the computation. The most common are the ReLU and sigmoid functions. Although rarely used in modern deep learning networks, a simple activation function is the step function. Let's look at the step function first, and then the ReLU and sigmoid functions.

Step function

Also known as the Heaviside function (Figure 21.6), a neuron with the step function as its activation function "activates" with a value of 1 if $z > 0$ – otherwise, it outputs the value 0.

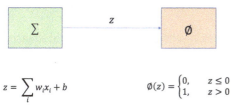

$$z = \sum_i w_i x_i + b$$

$$\emptyset(z) = \begin{cases} 0, & z \le 0 \\ 1, & z > 0 \end{cases}$$

Step Function (Heaviside) **Figure 21.6:** Step Function.

ReLU function

The most common activation function is the ReLU (Figure 21.7), or rectified linear unit. With ReLU, the output is 0 if $z \le 0$ – otherwise, it is the value z itself.

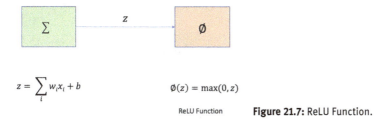

$$z = \sum_i w_i x_i + b$$

$$\emptyset(z) = \max(0, z)$$

ReLU Function **Figure 21.7:** ReLU Function.

$\phi(z) = max(0, z)$ is an elegant way of expressing the ReLU function: If the input is 0 or a negative number, the output is 0. If the input is a positive number, the output is the number itself.

Sigmoid function

Another common activation function is the sigmoid (Figure 21.8). It is commonly used when the output needs to estimate probabilities. The sigmoid is the familiar function of logistic regression.

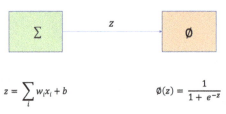

$$z = \sum_i w_i x_i + b \qquad\qquad \emptyset(z) = \frac{1}{1 + e^{-z}}$$

Sigmoid Function   **Figure 21.8:** Sigmoid Function.

We recall that the sigmoid function takes as an input any real number $\mathbb{R}$ and squashes it so it is in the range between 0 and 1.

21.1.1 Activation Function Computation

Now let's complete Step 2 for our example. In our example, as shown in Figure 21.9, the output $z = 1.06$ is fed as input to an activation function ϕ. Depending on the activation function, the resulting output (represented as a) is: 1, 1.06, or .74 for Heaviside, ReLU, and sigmoid functions, respectively.

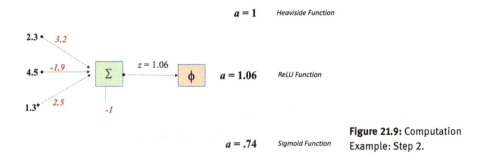

$a = 1$ Heaviside Function

$z = 1.06$

$a = 1.06$ ReLU Function

Figure 21.9: Computation Example: Step 2.

$a = .74$ Sigmoid Function

21.2 Mathematics of Neural Computation

We can represent the mathematics of a neuron's computation in the general case with the following set of equations.

Transfer Function

First, we take a linear combination of the weighted inputs plus the bias, calling it z. Once again, we should notice that the equation (with a change in notation) is exactly that of multiple regression.

$$z = \sum_{i=1}^{n} w_i x_i + b$$

Activation Functions

We pass the result z as an input to an activation function ϕ to obtain the final output y.

$$y = \phi(z)$$

The two most commonly used activation functions in deep learning are the sigmoid and ReLU functions:

$$\text{sigmoid}(z) = \frac{1}{1 + e^{-z}}$$
$$\text{ReLU}(z) = \max(0, z)$$

Combining Steps 1 and 2, the full function for neuron computation is:

$$y = \phi\left(\sum_{i=1}^{n} w_i x_i + b \right) \qquad (21.2)$$

21.3 Linear Algebra for Neural Computation

Computations in deep learning are performed using the tools of linear algebra, which are vectors and matrices. For neural computation, we will begin by working with vectors and then generalize more fully to matrices in later chapters. In this section, we review vectors and vector operations.

Most of us are familiar with functions. Up to first-year calculus, the functions f that we deal with associate *one* number $f(x)$ to *one* number x. This association is also called *mapping*. But in machine learning, and indeed in most advanced sciences, we need to go beyond mapping one number to another. The general idea of a function **f** is one which takes n numbers and returns m numbers. Both the input and output can be represented as lists or arrays of numbers.

We will call a one-dimensional array of numbers a *vector*. Each item or component in the array has an index. We will denote a vector in bold (**x**). By default, vectors will be expressed as columns. The following is an example of a vector:

$$\mathbf{x} = \begin{bmatrix} x_1 \\ x_2 \\ \vdots \\ x_n \end{bmatrix}$$

Now we define three common vector operations relevant to artificial neural networks: *scalar multiplication*, *vector addition* and *dot product*. A scalar is a single number. Multiplying a scalar (e. g., 5) with a vector yields another vector:

Scalar multiplication

$$5 \times \begin{bmatrix} x_1 \\ x_2 \\ \vdots \\ x_n \end{bmatrix} = \begin{bmatrix} 5 \times x_1 \\ 5 \times x_2 \\ \vdots \\ 5 \times x_n \end{bmatrix}$$

Vector addition

For vector addition, we simply add the elements of each vector.

$$\mathbf{x} + \mathbf{y} = \begin{bmatrix} x_1 + y_1 \\ x_2 + y_2 \\ \vdots \\ x_n + y_n \end{bmatrix}$$

A special case of vector addition is when we add a scalar to a vector. The result is a vector where scalar addition is "broadcast" to each element of the vector:

$$\mathbf{x} + a = \begin{bmatrix} x_1 + a \\ x_2 + a \\ \vdots \\ x_n + a \end{bmatrix}$$

Vector transpose

By default, vectors are represented as column vectors. But for some operations, we need to work with row vectors. Column vectors can be transformed to row vectors (and vice versa) using the transpose operator. If we start with a column vector,

$$\mathbf{x} = \begin{bmatrix} x_1 \\ x_2 \\ \vdots \\ x_n \end{bmatrix}$$

then its transpose is a row vector:

$$\mathbf{x}^\mathsf{T} = [x_1, x_2, \ldots, x_n]$$

Dot product

The dot product of two vectors **a** and **b** is defined as:

$$\mathbf{a} \cdot \mathbf{b} = a_1 b_1 + a_2 b_2 + \ldots + a_n b_n = \sum_{i=1}^{n} a_i b_i$$

Neural computation in vector form

We are now ready to write neural computation in vector form. If **x** represents the input vector and **w** the weight vector for a particular neuron, then neural computation can be expressed as:

$$y = \phi(\mathbf{w}^\mathsf{T} \cdot \mathbf{x} + b) \tag{21.3}$$

Returning to our earlier example, Figure 21.10 shows the computations for a particular neuron with three inputs and, therefore, three weights. Its activation function is sigmoid. Using vectors, we can write out the computation as:

$$z = \begin{bmatrix} 3.2 & -1.9 & 2.5 \end{bmatrix} \begin{bmatrix} 2.3 \\ 4.5 \\ 1.3 \end{bmatrix} - 1$$

$$y = \text{sigmoid}(z) = .74$$

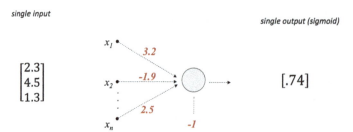

Figure 21.10: A neuron with three inputs and a sigmoid activation function. The weights for the input are: 3.2, −1.9, 2.5. The neuron's bias is: −1.

21.4 Neural Computation in Matrix Form

Thus far, we have expressed neural computation for a single input. But in machine learning, we often need to process inputs in batches. What if multiple training examples are sent to a neuron? In order to express the computation of a batch of inputs by a single neuron, we need to make use of matrices.

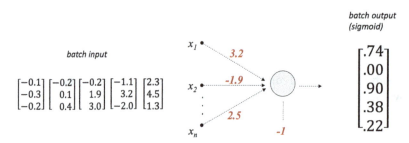

Figure 21.11: The same neuron and the resulting output when the input is a batch.

Figure 21.11 shows the same neuron as in Figure 21.10. However, this time we have a batch of five inputs. We will continue to use a vector **w** to represent a neuron's weights. However, the input can no longer be expressed by a vector **x**. Instead, we use the matrix **X** to signify the batch of inputs. Each row consists of a single input with three features. Each column is a different input example. Five rows means there are five inputs in the batch.

$$\mathbf{X} = \begin{bmatrix} 2.3 & 4.5 & 1.3 \\ -1.1 & 3.2 & -2.0 \\ -0.2 & 1.9 & 3.0 \\ -0.2 & 0.1 & 0.4 \\ -0.1 & -0.3 & -0.2 \end{bmatrix}$$

We are now ready to express neural computation for a batch of inputs in matrix form. In computing z (the output of the linear function), the weights vector remains as before. However, the input is no longer a vector $\mathbf{x}$, but the matrix $\mathbf{X}$. In addition, we have to transpose the matrix from $\mathbf{X}$ to $\mathbf{X}^\mathsf{T}$ to align rows and columns for matrix multiplication.

$$\mathbf{y} = \phi\left(\mathbf{w}^\mathsf{T} \cdot \mathbf{X}^\mathsf{T} + b\right) \tag{21.4}$$

$$z = \begin{bmatrix} 3.2 & -1.9 & 2.5 \end{bmatrix} \begin{bmatrix} 2.3 & -1.1 & -0.2 & -0.2 & -0.1 \\ 4.5 & 3.2 & 1.9 & -0.1 & -0.3 \\ 1.3 & -2.0 & 3.0 & 0.4 & -0.2 \end{bmatrix} - 1$$

Since there were five inputs in the batch, the resulting output is a vector with entries.

$$\mathbf{y} = \text{sigmoid}(z) = \begin{bmatrix} .74 \\ 0 \\ .90 \\ .38 \\ .22 \end{bmatrix}$$

21.5 Summary

In this chapter, we showed that an artificial neuron is a function that takes in one or more inputs to produce an output. The neuron's computation consists of two steps, each of which is a function. The first computation is linear: each input is multiplied by a weight, the resulting terms are summed, and then added to the bias. The second computation is non-linear. The output of the first computation is fed as an input to an activation function. Two common activation functions in deep learning are ReLU and sigmoid. Finally, we showed how neural computation can be performed using vectors and matrices.

22 Neurons – Practice

In this chapter, we program a neuron from scratch in Python. We use two approaches. For the first approach, we use define several functions. The principal function for performing the neuron's computation is called *neuron_output*. For the second approach, we define a *Neuron* class that bundles together the several functions.

Import Python libraries

First, we load the **numpy** library.

```python
import numpy as np
```

Neuron defined as a set of functions

Define input, weights, and bias
The input (x) will have three features. Therefore, the neuron will have three weights (w) and one bias (b). We explicitly define values for the input, the weights, and the bias.

```python
# define input as x
x = np.array([2.3,4.5,1.3])

# define weights as w
w = np.array([3.2,-1.9,2.5])

# define bias
b = np.array([-1])
```

Define activation functions
We define two possible activation functions for the neuron: ReLU and sigmoid.

```python
# define relu function
def relu(z):
    return np.maximum(z, 0)
```

https://doi.org/10.1515/9781501505737-022

```
# define sigmoid function
def sigmoid(z):
    return 1.0/(1.0 + np.exp(-z))
```

Define neuron's output function
The function *neuron_output* takes three inputs: *x*, *weights*, and *bias*. It calculates an output based on the data input and settings for the weights and biases.

```
# define neuron output function
def neuron_output(x,weights,bias,phi):
    z = np.dot(weights.T,x)+bias
    return phi(z)
```

Neuron output with ReLU as activation function

```
neuron_output(x,w,b,relu)
```

We calculate the output for a specific input and settings for weights and biases, but with activation function ReLU.
Output: 1.06

Neuron output with sigmoid as activation function
We calculate output with activation function sigmoid.

```
neuron_output(x,w,b,sigmoid)
```

Output: 0.74

Neuron class

Rather than write separate functions, we create a Neuron class.

Define input to the neuron
The input to the neuron will have three features. The input will also be a batch input, sending three input examples through the neuron.

```
# define input as X
X = np.array([[2.3,4.5,1.3],[-1.1,3.2,-2],[-.2,1.9,3]])
```

Create Neuron class

The *Neuron* class has an *init* method and a *calc_output* method.

```python
# create Neuron class
class Neuron:
    def __init__(self, neuron_input,weights,bias,activation_function):
        self.w = weights
        self.b = bias
        self.X = neuron_input
        self.phi = activation_function
    def calc_output(self):
        z = np.dot(w,X.T) + b
        a = np.round(self.phi(z),2)
        return a
```

Neuron output with ReLU as activation function

We instantiate the Neuron class with ReLU as activation function and then calculate the output. The input are three samples. Each sample has three features.

```python
# instantiate neuron class and calculate output for relu
Neuron_relu = Neuron(X,w.T,b,relu)
Neuron_relu.calc_output()
```

Output: [1.06, 0.0, 2.25]

Neuron output with sigmoid as activation function

We instantiate another neuron with sigmoid as the activation function and then calculate an output for the same input batch.

```python
# instantiate neuron class and calculate output for sigmoid
Neuron_sigmoid = Neuron(X,w.T,b,sigmoid)
Neuron_sigmoid.calc_output()
```

Output: [0.74, 0.0, 0.9]

23 Network Architecture

In the previous chapter, we considered a single neuron as the basic computational unit of deep learning. In this chapter, we examine the "network" part of artificial neural networks. The power of deep learning derives from the *organization* of neurons into *layers*. The purpose of this chapter is to gain an understanding of neural network architecture. By "neural architecture" we mean how neurons are organized for computation in a neural network.

Key Idea 1. In an artificial neural network (ANN), neurons are stacked vertically in *layers*.

Key Idea 2. In a feed-forward network, also called a multilayer perceptron (MLP), neurons are *densely connected*, meaning that each neuron in a layer receives an input from all the neurons in the previous layer and sends an output to every neuron in the next layer.

Key Idea 3. The first layer of a neural network is the *input layer*. It consists of data only. The last layer is the *output layer*, consisting of neurons responsible for producing the final output. The layers between the first and last layers are called the *hidden layers*.

23.1 Layers

A deep learning network consists of a series of neurons organized in vertical layers. For example, the neural network in Figure 23.1 consists of four layers with 3, 4, 2, 4 neurons in each of the layers. We use subscripts to uniquely identify each neuron in the network. The first subscript indicates the layer and the second subscript indicates its vertical position. For example, $N_{2,3}$ refers to the third neuron from the top in the second layer.

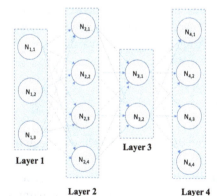

Figure 23.1: A neural network with 4 layers.

Every neural network also has an input and output layer. In between the input and output layers are one or more hidden layers.

https://doi.org/10.1515/9781501505737-023

Let's examine the neural network in Figure 23.2. The network has seven inputs in the input layer. The input layer consists of data only. There are no neurons. The number of inputs corresponds to the number of features used for prediction. The output layer contains two neurons. Therefore, there are two outputs (y_1 and y_2) for this particular network. Finally, there are two hidden layers consisting of three and four neurons. Note: Although the input layer is referred to as a layer, it is not counted as a layer in the network architecture. The number of layers in a neural network is the number of hidden layers plus the output layer.

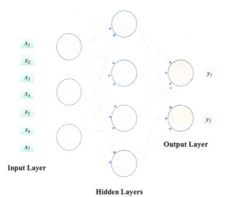

Figure 23.2: A neural network has three types of layers: input, hidden, and output.

Neurons in a neural network send messages to each other. The flow of the messages is determined by their connections. In a *generic* deep learning network, the neurons are *densely connected*, meaning that each neuron is connected to *every* neuron in the previous layer and to *every* neuron in the subsequent layer.

Figure 23.3 shows three layers of a neural network, containing 3, 4, and 2 neurons. $N_{2,3}$ in Layer 2 is densely connected, as are all neurons in the network. In other words, $N_{2,3}$ is connected to all three neurons in Layer 1 and both neurons in Layer 3. This means that $N_{2,3}$ receives or has three inputs from the previous layer and sends its output to both neurons in the subsequent layer.

23.2 Parameters

As we saw in the section on neurons, each neuron associates a weight with each input. Each neuron also has a bias. The weights and biases are the *parameters* associated with the neuron. The parameters are critically important in a deep learning network since their values have to be learned during the training process. Initially, the parameters are set arbitrarily – often randomly – to an initial set of values. As we shall see in the section on backward propagation, the parameter values (i. e., the weights and biases) are adjusted or learned during the training process.

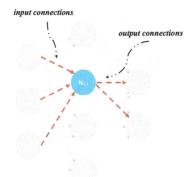

input connections

output connections

Figure 23.3: In a densely connected network each neuron receives inputs from all neurons in the previous layer and sends its output to all neurons in the next layer.

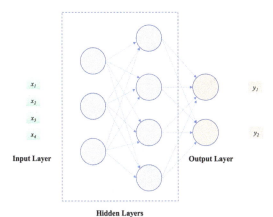

x_1

x_2

x_3

x_4

y_1

y_2

Input Layer

Output Layer

Hidden Layers

Figure 23.4: A simple network with 4 inputs in the input layer, 2 hidden layers, and an output layer with 2 neurons.

Our goal in this section is to count the total number of parameters in a neural network. We will start with a simple example and then generalize. Figure 23.4 shows a simple network with 4 inputs, 2 hidden layers (3 neurons in first layer, 4 neurons in second layer), and 2 neurons in the output layer. How many parameters are there in the network?

Let's look at the first layer and count its parameters. Figure 23.5 shows the calculation for the first neuron. The parameters of a single neuron are its weights and its bias. The number of weights is equal to the number of its inputs. Therefore, the number of parameters for each neuron in Layer 1 is 5. Since there are three neurons in Layer 1, the total number of parameters in Layer 1 is 15.

Figure 23.6 shows the parameter calculations for Layer 2. Once again, the number of parameters for a number equals the number of inbound inputs plus the bias. The number of parameters in the second layer is 16.

Finally, Figure 23.7 shows the total number of parameters in the network. There are 15 parameters in the first layer, 16 parameters in the second layer, and 10 parameters in the final output layer. The total number of parameters, therefore, is 41.

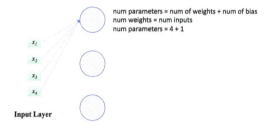

num parameters = num of weights + num of bias
num weights = num inputs
num parameters = 4 + 1

num parameters in layer = num of parameters per neuron × num of neurons in layer

num parameters in layer = 5 × 3 = 15

Figure 23.5: The number of parameters in the first layer is function of the number of inputs and the number of neurons. In the example, there are 4 inputs and 3 neurons. Each neuron has 5 parameters, since it has 4 weights (corresponding to the number of inputs) + 1 bias. Since there are 3 neurons, the total number of parameters is 15.

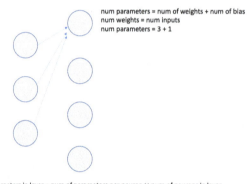

num parameters = num of weights + num of bias
num weights = num inputs
num parameters = 3 + 1

num parameters in layer = num of parameters per neuron × num of neurons in layer

num parameters in layer = 4 × 4 = 16

Figure 23.6: There are 16 parameters in the second layer. Each neuron has 4 parameters and there are 4 neurons in the layer.

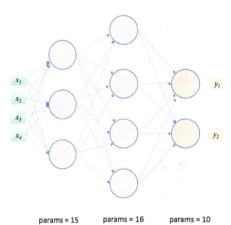

params = 15   params = 16   params = 10

Figure 23.7: The total number of parameters in the example network is 41.

We can now state the general formula for counting the total number of parameters in a neural network. Let $N_p(total)$ represent the total number of parameters and $N_p(\ell)$ is the number of parameters in some layer ℓ.

The number of parameters in a layer ℓ is the number of neurons in that layer $N_p(\ell)$ multiplied by the number of inputs to the layer plus the number of neurons in the layer.

$$N_p(\ell) = N_{neurons}(\ell) \times N_{inputs}(\ell) + N_{neurons}(\ell)$$

The total number of parameters is the sum of the parameters in each layer.

23.3 Hyperparameters

The weights and biases are the parameters of a neural network. Hyperparameters are the structural characteristics of the network, including the number of layers, the number of neurons in each layer, the particular activation functions, and other characteristics that we will see later, such as the loss and cost function. The values for the parameters are learned during the process of training. The values for the hyperparameters are set beforehand. The values for the hyperparameters are also "tuned" during model development in order to find the optimal configuration of the neural network for the task at hand.

23.4 Summary

In this chapter, we described the architecture of a feed-forward neural network as consisting of a set of vertical layers. Every network has an input and an output layer, and typically one or more hidden layers. In a feed-forward network the neurons are all densely connected. Finally, we described how to compute the number of parameters in the network.

24 Network Architecture – Practice

In this chapter, we use the **Keras** library to define a neural network. **Keras** is one of the most widely used deep learning frameworks for building and experimenting with deep learning models. **Keras** runs on top of **TensorFlow**.

Import Keras library

First, we import elements from the **Keras** library needed to build a neural network.

```
from keras import models
from keras import layers
```

Define neural network

The neural network called "model" will consist of an input layer, two hidden layers, and an output layer. The input shape is (13,), which means that the input will consist of 13 features.

The *Sequential* class in **Keras** allows us to build the network layer by layer. The first hidden layer is a dense network consisting of 64 neurons. Its input shape is 13. It will use ReLU as the activation function. The second hidden layer also consists of 64 neurons. It also uses ReLU as the activation function. The output layer will consist of a single neuron. Since we intend to use this network for regression, the output layer neuron does not need an activation function.

Once we have defined the neural network, we can proceed to compile it. The compilation step requires that we specify the optimizer type, the loss function and metrics to evaluate model accuracy. We use *rmsprop* (a widely used optimizer for regression) and *mse* (mean-squared error) as the loss function.

```
# Use Sequential API to create the network
model = models.Sequential()

# add the first hidden layer (64 neurons)
model.add(layers.Dense(64, activation='relu',
                         input_shape=(13,)))
# add the second hidden layer (64 neurons)
model.add(layers.Dense(64 ,activation='relu'))

# add the output layer (single neuron)
model.add(layers.Dense(1))
```

https://doi.org/10.1515/9781501505737-024

```
# compile the model
model.compile(optimizer="rmsprop", loss="mse", metrics=["mae","mse"])
```

Review model

```
model.summary()
```

We can review characteristics of the model just created by looking at the summary report shown in Figure 24.1. The report is also a quick way to see how many trainable parameters (weights, biases) are in each layer. The report confirms that a network was created with three layers. The first hidden layer contains 64 neurons. Its input shape is 13, meaning that there are 13 features in the input layer. There is a total of 896 parameters in the first layer.

The second hidden layer also has 64 neurons. The number of parameters in the second layer is 4160. Although the first and second layers contain the same number of neurons (i. e., 64), the number of parameters in the second layer is significantly higher. The reason is that there are 13 inputs to the first layer, while there are 64 inputs to the second layer.

Finally, the output layer consists of a single layer. It has 65 parameters since it receives 64 inputs from the second hidden layer. The network contains a total of 5,121 parameters.

```
Model: "sequential_4"
```

Layer (type)	Output Shape	Param #
dense_10 (Dense)	(None, 64)	896
dense_11 (Dense)	(None, 64)	4160
dense_12 (Dense)	(None, 1)	65

```
Total params: 5,121
Trainable params: 5,121
Non-trainable params: 0
```

Figure 24.1: Model summary of neural network.

25 Forward Propagation

Neurons are the basic building blocks of neural networks. In the last chapter, we saw how neurons are organized in vertical layers to form a network. Each neuron is connected to every neuron in the previous and next layers to form a densely connected network. In this chapter, our goal is to understand how computations are performed in each layer and then transmitted across the layers. This flow of computation from one layer to the next is called *forward propagation.*

Key Idea 1. Computation in a neural network propagates forward from the input layer to each of the hidden layers until it reaches the output layer.

Key Idea 2. Each layer can be represented as a mathematical function.

Key Idea 3. The computation from layer to layer can be represented by function composition.

Key Idea 4. The function part of each layer is expressed by a weights matrix.

25.1 Forward Propagation Flow

A falling rock disturbs a pond. The ripple fans out as waves which eventually reach the shore line. A generic neural network is a feed forward network. The input can be thought of as starting a ripple of *computation* that flows sequentially from left to right, through each layer without feedback or loops. The neural network receives an input, computes the input in the first layer to produce an output; the output of the first layer is then sent as an input to the second layer, which in turn produces an output and so on. The series of outputs is fed forward until the last layer is reached to produce the final output, as shown in Figure 25.1.

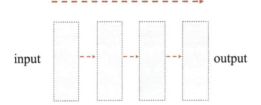

Figure 25.1: In a feed forward network computation flows sequentially through each of the layers to produce a final output.

25.2 Function Composition

A feed forward neural network is a chain of computations. Here we make an important leap in abstraction. Instead of worrying about individual computations of millions of neurons, we will regard the unit of computation as the layer and not the individual neuron.

https://doi.org/10.1515/9781501505737-025

Mathematically, we will represent the computation in each layer as a function: $f^{(1)}, f^{(2)}, f^{(3)}, \ldots$ The first layer receives an input a_0, performs the computation $f^{(1)}(a_0)$ to produce output a_1. Next, a_1 becomes the input to the next layer $f^{(2)}(a_1)$ to produce the output a_2, and so on. Each layer in a neural network is represented by a mathematical function, as shown in Figure 25.2.

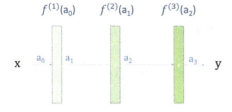

Figure 25.2: The computation in each layer can be represented by a function.

Previously, we introduced the idea of function composition. We note once again that when we express a chain of functions as function composition, the sequence of computation flows from inner to outer.

$$y = f^{(3)}(f^{(2)}(f^{(1)}(x)))$$

Order matters. The above function is not the same as the function below which computes f^3 first, then f^2, and finally f^1:

$$y = f^{(1)}(f^{(2)}(f^{(3)}(x)))$$

Let's look at a function composition example. Suppose we have two functions, $f(x)$ and $g(x)$:

$$f(x) = x + \pi$$

The first function $f(x)$ takes x as an argument and simply adds the constant π to x.

$$g(x) = sin(x)$$

The second function is the $sin(x)$ function from trigonometry. It takes x as an argument and produces as an output the sine of x.

We can build a more complex function $h(x)$ through function composition:

$$h(x) = g(f(x))$$

To compute $h(x)$, we substitute $f(x)$ in the function $g(x)$ to get:

$$h(x) = sin(x + \pi)$$

We can interpret the computation in $h(x)$ as occurring in two steps. First, we take some argument as x and add π to it. Second, we take the output of the first function and provide it as an input to the second function. The two steps are illustrated in Figure 25.3.

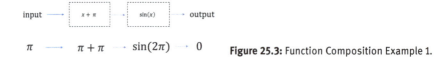

Figure 25.3: Function Composition Example 1.

Let's take a look at another function $i(x)$, composed of the same two functions $f(x)$ and $g(x)$ but in a different order:

$$i(x) = f(g(x))$$

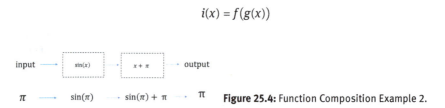

Figure 25.4: Function Composition Example 2.

Because the sequence of computations is different (as shown in Figure 25.4), the output for the same input π is different. In the first example, $h(\pi) = 0$. In the second example, $i(\pi) = \pi$.

25.3 Forward Propagation Computation

Let's work through an example with a simple neural work as shown in Figure 25.5. The neural network consists of 2 layers. The first layer, which is also the only hidden layer, consists of two neurons. The output layer consists of a single neuron. The activation function for the hidden layer is ReLU. The activation function for the output layer is sigmoid.

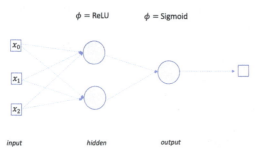

Figure 25.5: Forward-Propagation Example.

Let's look now at how we can represent such a network using vectors and matrices.

Input

Since the input has three features, we represent it as a vector with three rows.

$$\mathbf{x} = \begin{bmatrix} x_1 \\ x_2 \\ x_3 \end{bmatrix}$$

Layers: weights and biases

The first layer contains two neurons, each of which receive three inputs from the input layer. Therefore, its weights are represented by $W^{(1)}$, a 2×3 matrix. Each row represents a neuron, and the columns represent the neuron's associated weights. The weights for the final output layer are represented by $W^{(2)}$, a 1×2 matrix. The single row represents the sole neuron in the layer and the two columns represent weights associated with the two inputs from the previous layer.

$$W^{(1)} = \begin{bmatrix} w_{11} & w_{12} & w_{13} \\ w_{21} & w_{22} & w_{23} \end{bmatrix} \qquad W^{(2)} = \begin{bmatrix} w_{11} & w_{12} \end{bmatrix}$$

The biases for the two layers are $b^{(1)}$ and $b^{(2)}$.

$$b^{(1)} = \begin{bmatrix} b_{11} \\ b_{21} \end{bmatrix} \qquad b^{(2)} = \begin{bmatrix} b_{11} \end{bmatrix}$$

We are now ready to state the computation for forward propagation in matrix form. The computation for the first layer is:

$$\mathbf{A}^{(1)} = \text{ReLU}(\mathbf{W}^{(1)} \cdot \mathbf{A}^{(0)} + \mathbf{b}^{(1)})$$

Expressed in terms vectors and matrices:

$$\mathbf{A}^{(1)} = \text{ReLU}\left(\begin{bmatrix} w_{11} & w_{12} & w_{13} \\ w_{21} & w_{22} & w_{23} \end{bmatrix} \cdot \begin{bmatrix} x_1 \\ x_2 \\ x_3 \end{bmatrix} + \begin{bmatrix} b_{11} \\ b_{21} \end{bmatrix} \right)$$

We note that $\mathbf{A}^{(0)}$, the input into the first layer, is just the input vector $\mathbf{x}$. We also note that the activation function for the first layer is ReLU. The output of the computation is $\mathbf{A}^{(1)}$, which we now use as the input for computation of the second layer:

$$\mathbf{A}^{(2)} = \phi(\mathbf{W}^{(2)} \cdot \mathbf{A}^{(1)} + \mathbf{b}^{(2)})$$

Expressed as vectors and matrices, the computation for the second layer can be expressed as:

$$\mathbf{A}^{(2)} = \text{sigmoid}\left([w_{11} \quad w_{12}] \cdot \mathbf{A}^{(1)} + [b_{11}]\right)$$

We note that the activation function for the second layer is sigmoid.

The computations for forward propagation for the i-th layer can be written compactly as:

$$\mathbf{A}^{(l)} = \phi(\mathbf{W}^{(l)} \cdot \mathbf{A}^{(l-1)} + \mathbf{b}^{(l)}) \tag{25.1}$$

We place the indices in parentheses so they are not confused with exponents.

25.4 Computation Worked Example

Let's now work through an example to understand how the computations in forward propagation are performed. The network for the worked example is shown in Figure 25.6. The network consists of one hidden layer and an output layer consisting of a single neuron. The hidden layer consists of two neurons. The activation function for the hidden layer is ReLU. The activation function for the output layer is sigmoid. The sigmoid function is often used as the activation function in the output layer if the deep learning network's task is classification.

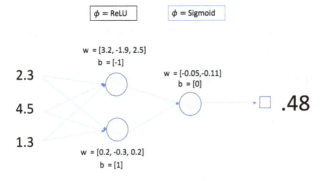

ϕ = ReLU ϕ = Sigmoid

w = [3.2, -1.9, 2.5]
b = [-1]

2.3

4.5

1.3

w = [0.2, -0.3, 0.2]
b = [1]

w = [-0.05,-0.11]
b = [0]

.48

Figure 25.6: A network with one hidden layer consisting of 2 neurons and an output layer with a 1 neuron. The activation function in the hidden layer is ReLU. The activation function in the output layer is sigmoid.

Input

For the worked example, the input into the neural network is the vector **x**. Each row represents a feature. We can imagine the network was setup to predict loan default. The network accepts three input features and then the output or prediction is a probability, similar to logistic regression.

$$\mathbf{x} = \begin{bmatrix} 2.3 \\ 4.5 \\ 1.3 \end{bmatrix}$$

Weights and biases

In a neural network, we represent each layer with a set of vectors and matrices. The weights of the two neurons in the hidden layer are stored in $W^{(1)}$. Each row represents a neuron. There are two rows in $W^{(1)}$, since there are two neurons in the hidden layer. The output layer has a single neuron. Its weights are stored in $W^{(2)}$. The biases of the two neurons are stored in $b^{(1)}$. The bias of the single vector in the output layer is stored in $b^{(2)}$.

$$W^{(1)} = \begin{bmatrix} 3.2 & -1.9 & 2.5 \\ 0.2 & -0.3 & 0.2 \end{bmatrix} \quad W^{(2)} = \begin{bmatrix} -0.05 & -0.11 \end{bmatrix}$$

$$b^{(1)} = \begin{bmatrix} -1 \\ 1 \end{bmatrix} \quad b^{(2)} = \begin{bmatrix} 0 \end{bmatrix}$$

Forward-Propagation computations

We are now ready to perform the computations for forward propagation. The first computation is performed by the first layer. It takes the input **X** (which we call $\mathbf{A}^{(0)}$) and produces an output $\mathbf{A}^{(1)}$.

$$\mathbf{A}^{(1)} = \text{ReLU}(\mathbf{W}^{(1)} \cdot \mathbf{A}^{(0)} + \mathbf{b}^{(1)})$$

$$\mathbf{A}^{(1)} = \text{ReLU}\left(\begin{bmatrix} 3.2 & -1.9 & 2.5 \\ 0.2 & -0.3 & 0.2 \end{bmatrix} \cdot \begin{bmatrix} 2.3 \\ 4.5 \\ 1.3 \end{bmatrix} + \begin{bmatrix} -1 \\ 1 \end{bmatrix} \right)$$

$$\mathbf{A}^{(1)} = \begin{bmatrix} 1.06 \\ 0.37 \end{bmatrix}$$

The output of the first computation is fed as input to the second computation:

$$\mathbf{A}^{(2)} = \phi(\mathbf{W}^{(2)} \cdot \mathbf{A}^{(1)} + \mathbf{b}^{(2)})$$

$$\mathbf{A}^{(2)} = \text{Sigmoid}\left(\begin{bmatrix} -0.05 & -0.11 \end{bmatrix} \cdot \begin{bmatrix} 1.06 \\ 0.37 \end{bmatrix} + \begin{bmatrix} 0 \end{bmatrix} \right)$$

The final output is:

$$\mathbf{A}^{(2)} = 0.48$$

25.5 Summary

In this chapter, we described the process of forward propagation. Computation of an input proceeds sequentially through each of the layers until it reaches the final output layer. Mathematically, the computation is represented as function composition. Finally, the entire computation can be represented with vectors and matrices.

26 Forward Propagation – Practice

In this chapter, we use Python to create network layers from scratch. The goal is to understand the computation involved in forward propagation. Each layer is created using a Python class called *Layer*. In addition to *init*, the class has two other methods: *update_params* and *forward*. The *update_params* method allows us to set new weights and biases for the layer. The *forward* method computes the output for the layer.

Import libraries

We import the **numpy** library.

```python
import numpy as np
```

Define activation functions

Define the sigmoid and ReLU activation functions.

```python
def sigmoid(z):
    return 1.0/(1.0 + np.exp(-z))


def relu(z):
    return np.maximum(z, 0)
```

Define class *Layer*

Define the class *Layer* with methods to update parameters and calculate the forward propagation output. Initial weights and biases are randomly assigned during initialization.

```python
class Layer:

    def __init__(self,n_inputs,n_neurons):
        np.random.seed(21)
        self.weights = np.random.randn(n_neurons,n_inputs)
        self.biases = np.zeros((n_neurons,1))

    def update_params(self,new_weights,new_biases):
```

https://doi.org/10.1515/9781501505737-026

```
        self.weights = new_weights
        self.biases = new_biases

    def forward(self,inputs,phi):
        self.outputs = phi(np.dot(self.weights,inputs)+self.biases)
        return self.outputs
```

Create input values and parameters for Layer1

We create input values to test the computation. We will also set values for the weights and biases for the layer.

```
x1 = np.array([[2.3,4.5,1.3]])
x1 = x1.T
```

```
W1 = np.array([[3.2,-1.9,2.5],[.2,-.3,.2]])
b1 = np.array([[-1],[1]])
```

Instantiate first and second layers

We create Layer 1 with 3 inputs and 2 neurons. We create Layer 2 with 2 inputs (from Layer 1) and a 1 neuron.

```
L1 = Layer(3,2)
L2 = Layer(2,1)
```

Update parameters for Layer 1

We update the weights of Layer 1 using the values defined above in $W1$ and $b1$.

```
L1.update_params(W1,b1)
```

Calculate output for Layers 1 and 2

As part of the output, Layer 1 uses the ReLU activation function and Layer2 uses the sigmoid activation function.

```
A1 = L1.forward(x1,relu)
A2 = L2.forward(A1,sigmoid)
```

```
print(A2)
```

0.48

Multiple inputs and three layers

We now define a network with three layers, not counting the input layer. The first layer has 4 neurons, each of which receives three inputs. The second layer has 4 neurons, The final layer has 3 neurons.

Instantiate three layers

```
L1 = Layer(3,4)
L2 = Layer(4,4)
L3 = Layer(4,3)
```

Calculate output for Layers 1, 2, and 3
Calculate output for each layer. The first and second layer use ReLU as the activation function. The output layer uses softmax.

```
A1 = L1.forward(x1,relu)
A2 = L2.forward(A1,relu)
A3 = L3.forward(A2,softmax)A3
```

```
print(A3)
```

[[0.13] [0.07] [0.8]]

Input a batch
We now define a batch of five inputs.

```
X = np.array([[2.3,4.5,1.3],[.3,-2.2,2.1],
              [.6,.51,.63],[.23,-.45,1.1],[5.3,2.5,3.3]])
X = X.T
```

We apply forward propagation through the three layers for the batch and print the result.

```
A1 = L1.forward(X,relu)
A2 = L2.forward(A1,relu)
A3 = L3.forward(A2,softmax)

print(A3.T)

    ([
    [0.13, 0.07, 0.80],
    [0.70, 0.01, 0.30],
    [0.27, 0.13, 0.60],
    [0.39, 0.05, 0.56],
    [0.07, 0.00, 0.93]
    ])
```

27 Loss Function

In the last chapter, we saw that in a feed-forward neural network, data flows through a sequence of vertical layers. Input data is fed into the first layer for computation. The result is fed as the input to the second layer for further computation. The series of computations continues until the last layer produces a final output. In this chapter, we describe what occurs at the end of forward propagation: the neural network estimates its own accuracy or error. The estimate is quantified using a *loss function*. The error is then used to adjust the network parameters during backward propagation. The cycle of forward propagation, error estimate, and backward propagation repeats itself until the network reaches an acceptable level of accuracy.

Key Idea 1. Each pass of the data in forward propagation produces an output. The output is compared to the baseline truth for accuracy.

Key Idea 2. The *loss function* quantifies the accuracy or error for a single data pass. The *cost function* quantifies the accuracy or error for the entire dataset.

Key Idea 3. The goal of learning in deep learning is to adjust the parameters of the neural network such that the cost function is minimized.

27.1 A Game of Arrows

To motivate the discussion of loss and cost function, let's consider a game of arrows. Imagine we are judges at an archery competition. How do we determine the winner? We measure the accuracy of each shot, aggregate the scores for each participant, and rank the results. In machine learning, shot accuracy, the accuracy of an individual shot, is called "loss" and is measured by a loss function. The overall accuracy or aggregate score of a shooter is called "cost". Sometimes, the terms are used synonymously. What is important is that the network needs a formal mechanism to determine its performance before it can make any adjustments.

How do we measure shot accuracy in a game of arrows? By measuring the *distance* of the shot from the target. An arrow that hits the bullseye is perfectly accurate. Any deviation from the target is the "loss." Suppose Katniss Everdeen (heroine from *Hunger Games*) is in an archery competition with two other competitors, Odair and Abernathy. The competition consists of shooting ten arrows. The winner is the most accurate shooter. Table 27.1 is a record of the shooting competition. The loss function computes the error for a single shot. The cost averages the errors. Everdeen's more accurate shooting performance wins the game of arrows.

https://doi.org/10.1515/9781501505737-027

Table 27.1: Game of Arrows competition results.

Shot Number	Everdeen (Loss)	Odair (Loss)	Abernathy (Loss)
1	3	2	1
2	3	1	2
3	0	3	0
4	2	1	1
5	4	0	0
6	1	2	2
7	2	5	3
8	1	4	5
9	0	4	4
10	0	3	0
Cost (Mean)	1.6	2.5	1.8

27.2 Common Loss Functions in Deep Learning

A loss function in machine learning is based on an idea similar to the game of arrows. Each shot or a single input is assessed for accuracy against a known target. At the end of forward propagation, the output ($\hat{y}$) is evaluated against the desired output (y). The discrepancy between the two is the error. The most commonly used loss functions (Figure 27.1) in deep learning are: mean squared error, binary cross-entropy, and categorical cross-entropy.

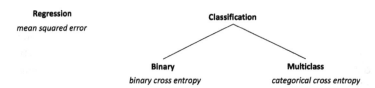

Figure 27.1: For regression problems in Deep Learning, the typical loss function is Mean Squared Error. For classification problems, the typical loss function for binary classification is binary cross entropy and for multiclass classification it's categorical cross entropy.

Let's look at how *Loss* is calculated in each. We will examine three deep learning networks. The first network, shown in Figure 27.2, predicts housing prices. The network has multiple features and the goal is to predict housing price based on the features. The model type is regression since the output is continuous. Regression models in deep learning typically use mean squared error as the loss function.

The second network, shown in Figure 27.3, predicts fraudulent transactions. The model receives a set of inputs regarding a transaction and predicts a binary outcome: fraud or not fraud. Binary classification models in deep learning typically use binary cross entropy as the loss function.

Regression

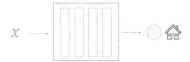

x

Goal: Predict Housing Price

Figure 27.2: The goal of the first deep learning network example is to predict housing price.

Binary Classification

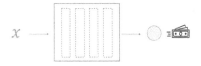

x

Goal: Predict Fraudulent Transaction

Figure 27.3: The goal of the second deep learning network example is to predict fraudulent transactions.

The third network, shown in Figure 27.4, classifies images as belonging to one of three categories: cats, dogs, or horses. The model type is multiclass classification. Multiclass classification models in deep learning typically use categorical cross entropy as the loss function.

The loss function for each network is different. Let's see how *Loss* is calculated for each.

Multi-Class Classification

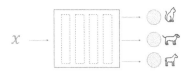

x

Goal: Predict image as belonging to one of three classes

Figure 27.4: The goal of the third deep learning network example is to classify images into one of three categories.

Mean Squared Error

Our first network is used to solve a regression problem. Let's suppose that for a particular input of the data, as shown in Figure 27.5, the predicted output $\hat{y}$ is 125,332 and the desired output (y) is 13,817. To calculate the "loss", we use mean squared error.

$\hat{y}$ y

prediction   true target

We have already seen mean squared error (MSE) and know how to calculate it. The loss for an individual prediction is the squared distance between the true target (y) and the prediction ($\hat{y}$):

$$L(y, \hat{y}) = (y - \hat{y})^2 \qquad (27.1)$$

In our example, the loss is calculated as:

$$L = (132{,}817 - 125{,}332)^2 = (7{,}485)^2 = 56{,}025{,}225$$

Categorical Cross-Entropy

Our second network involves multi-class classification. Figure 27.6 shows a neural network whose task is to classify pictures into one of three categories: cat, dog, or horse.

Accordingly, the output layer has three neurons. The output layer also uses *softmax* as the activation function in order to normalize the probabilities.

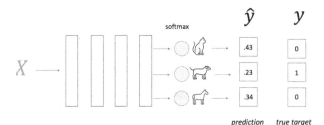

$\hat{y}$ y

prediction   true target

Figure 27.6: Categorical Cross-Entropy Example.

In classification, the value of $\hat{y}$ is always a probability ranging from 0 to 1. The desired outcome or target y is always either 0 or 1. Continuing with the example in Figure 27.6, let's suppose we send the image of dog as input to the neural network. The network's output or prediction is: $\hat{y}$ = [.43, .23, .34]. The prediction can be interpreted as: the probability of the picture being a cat is .43; the probability of it being a dog is .23; and the probability of it being a horse is .34.

For multiclass classification, the labels are prepared using one-hot encoding. In this example, the picture is that of a dog. The true target vector, therefore, is: $y = [0, 1, 0]$.

Let's now calculate the loss for this example. Before looking at the formula, we need to keep in mind that we only need to look at the true label in order to calculate the loss. In our example, the true label is a dog. And the prediction is a probability of .23. The formula is:

$$L = -y \cdot log(\hat{y})$$

Since y of the true target is 1 and $\hat{y} = .23$, the loss is:

$$L = -1 \cdot log(.23) = -log(.23) = 1.47$$

The general formula for calculating *Loss* for a single input is:

$$L(y_i, \hat{y}_i) = -\sum_{i=1}^{C_n} y_i \cdot log(\hat{y}_i) \tag{27.2}$$

In the formula, C_n is the number of classes. In our example, the number of classes is 3.

$$L = -(0 \cdot log(.43) + 01 \cdot log(.23) + 0 \cdot log(.35))$$

We should notice that only one of the three terms survive, namely the one that corresponds to the true target. Therefore, we only have to calculate the term that corresponds to the true target.

Binary Cross-Entropy

Our third network is for binary classification. For example, we might have set up a neural network to predict fraudulent transactions.

ŷ   y

.75   1

prediction   *true target*

Figure 27.7: Binary Cross-Entropy Example, Label = 1.

Figure 27.7 shows an example where the prediction for a transaction is .75. The transaction is indeed fraudulent with $y = 1$. The formula for calculating loss is:

$$L = -y \cdot log(\hat{y}) + (1 - y) \cdot log(1 - \hat{y})$$

In the case where the true target is 1, the formula reduces to $-log(\hat{y})$.

$$L = -log(\hat{y}) = -log(.75) = .29$$

Figure 27.8: Binary Cross-Entropy Example, Label = 0.

Let's now consider the case where the transaction is not fraudulent (i. e., $y = 0$). Figure 27.8 shows an example of a non-fraudulent transaction with a prediction score of .25. If the label is 0, then the formula reduces to $log(1 - \hat{y})$. We calculate the loss, therefore, as:

$$L = (1 - y) \cdot log(1 - \hat{y}) = log(1 - .25) = log(.75) = -.29$$

27.3 Summary

In this chapter, we described what occurs at the end of forward propagation. The neural network makes an estimate of the error using a loss function. We then described three common loss functions: mean squared error, binary cross entropy, and categorical cross entropy. We then showed how to calculate the loss function with some examples.

28 Loss Function – Practice

In this chapter, we define the three major loss functions used in Deep Learning. The functions are defined from scratch in Python so we can understand the underlying computation. The loss functions are: Mean-Squared Error (MSE), Categorical Cross-Entropy, and Binary Cross Entropy.

Import libraries

We import the **numpy** library.

```
import numpy
```

MSE Loss Function

We define *mse* as the loss function for regression tasks.

```
# define mean squared error loss function
def mse(y_hat,y):
    return np.sum((y_hat - y)**2)/len(y)
```

We define inputs to the function. $\hat{y}$ is the prediction. y is the true value.

```
# prediction
y_hat=np.array([0.6])

# true target
y = np.array([1.3])
```

The function mse calculates the loss based on *y_hat* and *y* as inputs.

```
mse(y_hat,y)
```

The result or loss is: **0.49**

Categorical Cross-Entropy Loss Function

We define categorical cross-entropy loss function for mult-class classification tasks. The function takes y and $\hat{y}$ has inputs.

https://doi.org/10.1515/9781501505737-028

```python
def cce(y_hat,y):
    return -np.dot(np.log(y_hat),y)
```

The input $\hat{y}$ is the prediction. In multi-class classification the prediction is a vector whose size is the number of categories. The values of the vector are the respective probabilities for each category. In the input below, the model predicts that the probability for category one is 0.1, for category two is 0.3, for category three is 0.4, and for category four is 0.2.

The true target is one-hot-encoded vector. In the input below, the true target is category two. It has the value 1, whereas the other categories have a value of 0.

```python
# predictions - four categories
y_hat = np.array([0.1, 0.3, 0.4, 0.2])

# true target, one-hot-encoded
y = np.array([0, 1, 0, 0])
```

We calculate categorical cross entropy for predication and true target.

```python
cce(y_hat,y)
```

The result is: **1.20**

Binary Cross-Entropy Function

We define binary cross-entropy function for binary classification tasks.

```python
def bce(y_hat, y):
    if y == 1:
        return -np.log(y_hat)
    else:
        return -np.log(1 - y_hat)
```

We define input values for calculating binary cross-entropy. In this example, the model predicts a probability of .2. The true target is 0.

```python
y_hat = np.array([.2])
y = np.array([0])
```

We calculate binary cross-entropy based on the above values.

```
bce(y_hat,y)
```

The result is: **0.22**

We define new input values. The probability is still .2. The true target is now 1.

```
y_hat = np.array([.2])
y = np.array([1])
```

We calculate binary cross-entropy based on the new values.

```
bce(y_hat,y)
```

The result is: **1.61**

29 Backward Propagation

In this chapter, we describe the crown jewel of deep learning. Backpropagation is the *learning* part of deep learning. We have seen how prediction begins with forward propagation, which takes an input and transforms it through successive layers of the neural network. We then saw how a loss function evaluates each prediction for accuracy. The final step is backpropagation, which takes the loss and adds its own calculation. The backpropagation optimizer calculates the incremental amount by which the weights and biases of the network need to be adjusted. The optimizer then adjusts the parameters from the last layer to the first layer. The cycle of forward and backward propagation occurs multiple times until the error rate diminishes to an acceptable level.

Key Idea 1. A neural network performs its computation using the weight and bias settings of neurons.

Key Idea 2. An optimizer adjusts values of the network parameters by calculating and applying gradients, a process called *gradient descent*.

Key Idea 3. The optimizer updates the parameters backwards, from the final layer to the first layer.

Key Idea 4. Forward and backward propagation algorithms proceed in cycles or *epochs* until the network reaches an acceptable level of predictive accuracy. A single epoch is the complete computation of an entire batch of inputs.

29.1 Computation as Gears

We began our study of machine learning with simple linear regression (SLR). We noted that the essence of supervised machine learning is prediction and it is computed by a function. In SLR, there are only two parameters: the slope (β_1) and the intercept (β_0). Fitting a model to the data means finding specific values for the two parameters. Computing the prediction, the output $\hat{y}$, consists of multiplying the input x by β_1 and adding β_0 to the result.

We can view the two parameters as mechanical gears (Figure 29.1) and their specific values as gear settings. The process of learning is discovering the optimal gear settings for the function computation to take place.

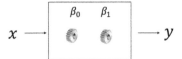

Figure 29.1: Simple Linear Regression has two parameters.

By contrast, a deep learning network (Figure 29.2) can have thousands, even millions of parameters. The parameters correspond to the weights and biases of the individual

https://doi.org/10.1515/9781501505737-029

neurons in the network. We saw that in forward propagation the neural network computes an output based on a set of inputs. At the end of each forward pass the network then evaluates the accuracy of the computation against a loss function. We arrive now at the final stage. The process of backpropagation is the process of learning the correct "gear setting" for each network parameter.

Figure 29.2: A Deep Learning network can have thousands, if not millions, of parameters.

29.2 Gradient Descent

In the case of simple linear regression, we have at our disposal a formula for calculating the two parameter values. Finding the values of the two parameters is simply a matter of plugging in values into a simple formula. But no such formula exists for deep learning networks. In such cases, we have to resort to a numerical solution.

Gradient descent is the most popular optimization algorithm for numerically estimating the values of the parameters of a deep learning network. First, let's see how it works intuitively.

Let's imagine that a mountaineer is stuck at the top of a mountain. It's nightfall and the mountaineer needs to descend as quickly as possible to the valley below. Because it's pitch black, the quickest route down is not visible. What is the mountaineer to do?

Figure 29.3: Gradient descent is analogous to taking small steps down a mountain path.

Fortunately, the mountaineer has a flashlight. By shining the flashlight in a circle, the mountaineer scans to see which direction steeps downward the quickest. The mountaineer navigates downward by alternatively shining her flashlight, finding the path of steepest descent, and taking steps in that direction. The process continues until she reaches the bottom as shown in Figure 29.3.

In the language of calculus and machine learning, the direction of steepest descent or ascent is called the "gradient." The gradient is also the slope. Mountaineers calculate gradients visually, but gradients can also be discerned from topographical or contour maps. Far apart contour lines indicate a gentle slope, while close contour lines indicate a steep slope.

In vector calculus, the gradient of a function f, evaluated at some point (x), is a vector that points in the direction of steepest ascent. Similarly, the negative gradient points in the direction of steepest descent. In our mountaineering analogy, *gradient descent* means descending stepwise along the *steepest path*.

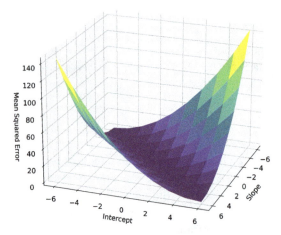

Figure 29.4: MSE Cost Function.

Gradient descent in machine learning, including deep learning, works similarly, but the mountain we are descending is the "mountain of error." The goal is to climb down the mountain of error as quickly as possible.

We saw in the last chapter that at the end of forward propagation, a neural network calculates the loss or error. We can think of the error as the mountain peak, and the goal of gradient descent is to navigate down to the least error (the bottom) as quickly as possible.

Figure 29.4 shows, for example, Mean Squared Error as a cost function in the case of simple linear regression. MSE is a function of the slope and the intercept. The line of best fit, the regression line, has the lowest MSE. But different combinations of the slope (m) and intercept (b) yield different values for the MSE. Applying gradient descent entails going down the MSE mountain until we reach the minimum for MSE.

Figure 29.5 is a two-dimensional representation of the gradients corresponding to the MSE cost function in Figure 29.4. The gradient vectors have both a magnitude and a direction. The direction of the vectors points to the direction of steepest descent. The size of the vector indicates the slope of the descent. At the top of the MSE "mountain," the arrows are larger and the descent is steeper. The arrows decrease in size as we descend down the MSE mountain.

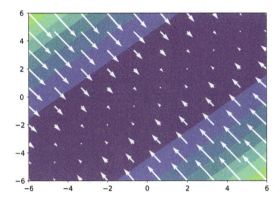

Figure 29.5: Gradient Vectors.

29.3 Gradient Descent for Simple Linear Regression

Now that we have a conceptual understanding of gradient descent, let's apply it in a simple case. Our first example of machine learning was simple linear regression. As a review, consider the set of points shown in Figure 29.6.

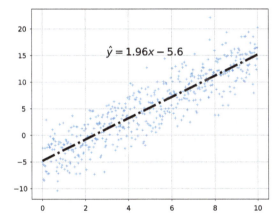

$$\hat{y} = 1.96x - 5.6$$

Figure 29.6: Simple Linear Regression.

There is a variety of software available for calculating the regression line or the line of best fit. But we saw that the line of best fit is the one that minimizes the squares of the residuals. We also saw that a formula is readily available for estimating the slope and intercept. With our mountaineering analogy, it would be equivalent to a mountaineer climbing down the mountain in daylight with full visibility of the "global" best path for descent. But let's assume that even in the case of simple linear regression, we did not have an "analytic" solution. Can we use gradient ascent to estimate values for the slope and intercept? The answer is yes. Let's see how we can apply stochastic gradient descent to simple linear regression.

The steps are as follows.

Gradient Descent for Simple Linear Regression.
- **Step 1**: Begin by guessing an initial estimate for the weight and the bias: (w, b). The weight is the slope and the bias is the intercept of the regression line. The guess can be to assign random values for both.
- **Step 2**: Compute the prediction $\hat{y}$ using the estimated slope and intercept.
- **Step 3**: Apply a loss function $L(y, \hat{y})$ to compute the loss or discrepancy between the target value (y) and the prediction (y_hat).
- **Step 4**: Using the loss, calculate the gradients for weight and bias: (dw, db)
- **Step 5**: Deduct the gradients from weights and biases to get new weights and biases:
    - $w = lr \times (w - dw)$
    - $b = lr \times (b - db)$
- Repeat the above steps until we reach the minimum.

We highlight a couple of points about gradient descent. First, we are assuming that there is a single minimum for the loss function. But not all functions have a single minimum. Returning to our mountaineering analogy, gradient descent guarantees that we reach a valley (a local minimum), not that we reached the bottom of the mountain (global minimum). Depending on the machine learning problem, this is one area where choice of the loss function matters.

The second comment concerns Step 5. In updating the weight, we calculated the gradient (dw) and subtracted it from the current weight to get the new weight. But we smuggled in a factor (lr) and applied it to $(w - dw)$. What is lr? It stands for learning rate. Recall that the gradient gives us the magnitude and direction of steepest ascent. Its negative gives us the magnitude and direction of steepest descent. One of the dangers, as we descend, is that we will overshoot the minimum as we approach it. The learning rate is a hyperparameter to allow optimal "steps" for approaching the minimum.

Let's now apply gradient descent to estimate the parameters for a simple linear regression problem. We set up a neural network with a single neuron and no activation function. Recall that a single neuron during the first step computes a weighted sum of its inputs and adds a bias. But that is linear regression.

Figure 29.7 shows various estimates of the slope and bias through a number of cycles of forward and backward propagation.

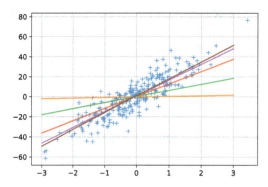

Figure 29.7: Estimates of the regression line using gradient descent.

Figure 29.7 displays estimates of the regression line where the neuron is fed input in batches of 10. If we change the batch size to 1, the network converges to an excellent estimate almost immediately. This is shown in Figure 29.8.

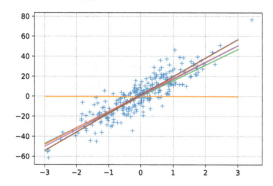

Figure 29.8: Estimates of the regression line using a different batch size.

In gradient descent (GD) the optimizer updates the weights (and biases) after each epoch. An epoch is an entire pass over the training dataset. In stochastic gradient descent (SGD) the optimizer updates the weights (and biases) after each training example. An intermediate approach evaluates the loss after each batch, where the batch size can be set as a hyperparameter. Depending on the size of the dataset and the nature of the deep learning problem, there are advantages and disadvantages to each approach.

29.4 Gradients and Backpropagation

We have given an example of how gradient ascent works for a single neuron. It begins with calculation of loss, the discrepancy between the true target value and the predicted value. From the loss value, the optimizer calculates gradients for the weights and biases. The gradients are then used to adjust the weights and biases of the network.

But a neural network can contain thousands and even millions of neurons. Backpropagation needs to adjust the parameters for each and every neuron. It involves calculating gradients for each layer, proceeding backwards through the network from the last layer through to the first.

Calculating the gradient at each layer requires using the *chain rule* of calculus to take partial derivatives. For those with a background in multi-variable calculus, we give details of the chain rule at the book's web site.

For our purposes, a conceptual understanding of the chain rule is sufficient. In our discussion of forward propagation, we noted that the computation of prediction can be represented formally as function composition:

$$f^{(n)}(f^{(n-1)}(\ldots f^{(2)}(f^{(1)}(X))))$$

The forward computation takes places in sequence from inner function $f^{(1)}$ to the last outer function $f^{(n)}$, where n represents the number of hidden and output layers of the network.

The backward computation also takes place in sequence, but in reverse order from outer function to the first inner function. The functions involved in backpropagation are functions for calculating gradients. Gradients of functions are represented as $\nabla f^{(n)}$, $\nabla f^{(n-1)}, \ldots, \nabla f^{(1)}$. The nabla symbol ∇, written as an upside-down triangle and pronounced "del," denotes the vector differential operator.

Applied to functions, the gradient of a differentiable function f of several variables yields a vector field. The vector field's value at a point $p = (x_1, x_2, \ldots, x_n)$ is the vector whose components are the partial derivatives of f at p.

$$\nabla f(x_1, x_2, \ldots, x_n) = \begin{bmatrix} \frac{\partial f}{\partial x_1}(x_1, x_2, \ldots, x_n) \\ \frac{\partial f}{\partial x_2}(x_1, x_2, \ldots, x_n) \\ \vdots \\ \frac{\partial f}{\partial x_n}(x_1, x_2, \ldots, x_n) \end{bmatrix}$$

Figure 29.5 shows a vector field associated with the Mean Squared Loss function. For our purposes, the details are less important than the bedrock principle that backpropagation calculates gradients and then applies the calculations to adjust the parameters of the neural network.

29.5 Summary

In this chapter, we discussed the final step of computation in neural networks. The purpose of a neural network is prediction. Its basic unit is a neuron, which is also the basic unit of computation. Neurons are organized in layers. During forward propagation, input data is transformed through the layers to produce an output prediction. The loss function evaluates the accuracy of the prediction against the true target. The error is then passed on to an optimizer, which calculates the gradients (i. e., changes) that need to applied to each parameter. The gradients are applied incrementally through multiple cycles of forward and backward propagation until the network achieves an acceptable level of accuracy.

30 Backward Propagation – Practice

In this chapter, we provide code for performing simple linear regression from scratch using gradient descent. Our aim is to understand how gradient descent works in the case of a very simple model. We begin by generating sample data. Then we use **scikit-learn** to perform the regression. Next, we use gradient descent to perform the regression. We then compare the results.

Import libraries

We import **numpy, matplotlib**, and *LinearRegression* from **scikit-learn**.

```
import numpy as np
import matplotlib.pyplot as plt

from sklearn.linear_model import LinearRegression
```

Generate sample data

We generate sample data for linear regression. The data includes noise. Roughly, the dataset has a slope of 2 and an intercept of –5.

```
x = np.linspace(0,10,500)

e = np.random.randn(500)

y = (2*x -5)+3*e
```

Perform regression with scikit-learn

We will run linear regression with **scikit-learn** as the first point of comparison.

```
x = x.reshape(-1,1)
y = y.reshape(-1,1)
lr = LinearRegression().fit(x, y)
```

We review the results of the regression. The coefficient (slope) is 1.93 and the intercept is –4.58. A plot of the data points and the regression line (as estimated by **scikit-learn**) is shown in Figure 30.1.

https://doi.org/10.1515/9781501505737-030

```
print(lr.coef_)
print(lr.intercept_)
```

```
plt.plot(x,y_pred,linewidth=5,linestyle="-.",c="black")
```

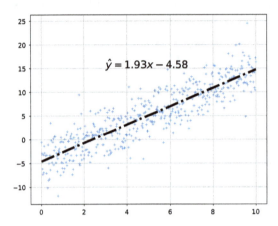

$\hat{y} = 1.93x - 4.58$

Figure 30.1: Plot of regression line generated by scikitlrn.

Perform regression using gradient descent

In order to perform simple linear regression using gradient descent, we define a *Neuron* class. Simple linear regression will be performed by a single neuron. The *init* method generates random values for slope and intercept. An empty list is created to track mean squared error through the iterations.

The principal method is an epoch. Each epoch performs a forward propagation computation for the entire dataset. A loss function (mean squared error) computes the loss for each example. Gradients are calculated, and then weights and biases are updated. The backpropagation step is simple in that only two parameters (single weight – single bias) have to be updated.

```
class Neuron:
    def __init__(self,inputs):

        # generate random values for weights and biases

        self.w = np.random.randn(inputs)
        self.b = np.random.randn(inputs)

        self.learn_rate = 0.01
```

```
        self.mse = []
        self.parameters = [[self.b,self.w]]

    def epoch(self,X,y):

        samples = len(X)

        # loop through the entire dataset

        for i in range(samples):
            sum_error = 0

            # calculate output
            y_hat = self.w*X[i] + self.b

            # calculate cost, update current loss
            error = y_hat - y[i]
            sum_error = error**2

            # calculate gradients
            dw = self.learn_rate * error * X[i]
            db = self.learn_rate * error

            # adjust parameters
            self.w = self.w - dw
            self.b = self.b - db

        # add mse for epoch to mse list
        self.mse.append(sum_error/len(X))
        self.parameters.append([self.b,self.w])

    def epochs(self,n_epochs,X,y):
        for n in range(n_epochs):
            self.epoch(X,y)
        return self.w, self.b
```

Instantiate neuron

We instantiate a single neuron and call it *n*. We run 25 epochs and print the resulting estimates of the slope and intercept. The slope estimate is 2.12 and the intercept estimate is –4.79. Both are fairly close to the estimates returned by **scikit-learn.** The regression line estimates by gradient descent are shown in Figure 30.2.

```
n = Neuron(1)
result = n.epochs(25,x,y)
print(result )
```

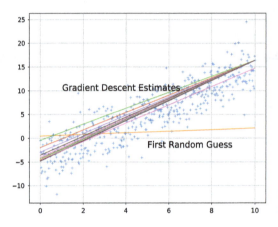

Figure 30.2: Regression line estimates by gradient descent.

31 Deep Learning – Practice

In this chapter, we use the **Keras** library to set up a simple deep learning network to run multiple regression. The "Wine Quality" dataset is from the UCI Machine Learning Repository and consists of various features associated with red and white vinho verde wine samples from the north of Portugal. The original two datasets (red and white) have been combined into a single dataset for purposes of the exercise.

Load libraries

First, we load the **pandas** library and functions from the **scikit-learn** and **keras** libraries.

```python
import pandas as pd

from sklearn.preprocessing import StandardScaler
from sklearn.model_selection import train_test_split
from sklearn.metrics import r2_score


from keras.models import Sequential
from keras.layers import Dense
```

Load and prepare dataset

We load the dataset as a pandas dataframe *df*.

```python
df = pd.read_csv('wines.csv')
df.head()
df.info()
```

The first few records of the dataset are displayed in Figure 31.1. The columns contain a variety of features related to each wine. The column 'type' is 1 or 0, where 1 means red wine and 0 means white wine. The quality of the wine is indicated in the 'quality' column.

Basic information about the dataset is shown in Figure 31.2. The dataframe consists of 6497 rows and 13 columns. All values are non-null.

In the next few lines we set up *X* and *y* as separate variables. *X* will contain all the feature variables and *y* will contain the target variable, *quality*.

https://doi.org/10.1515/9781501505737-031

	fixed acidity	volatile acidity	citric acid	residual sugar	chlorides	free sulfur dioxide	total sulfur dioxide	density	pH	sulphates	alcohol	quality	type
0	7.4	0.70	0.00	1.9	0.076	11.0	34.0	0.9978	3.51	0.56	9.4	5	1
1	7.8	0.88	0.00	2.6	0.098	25.0	67.0	0.9968	3.20	0.68	9.8	5	1
2	7.8	0.76	0.04	2.3	0.092	15.0	54.0	0.9970	3.26	0.65	9.8	5	1
3	11.2	0.28	0.56	1.9	0.075	17.0	60.0	0.9980	3.16	0.58	9.8	6	1
4	7.4	0.70	0.00	1.9	0.076	11.0	34.0	0.9978	3.51	0.56	9.4	5	1

Figure 31.1: First few records of wine quality dataset.

```
<class 'pandas.core.frame.DataFrame'>
RangeIndex: 6497 entries, 0 to 6496
Data columns (total 13 columns):
fixed acidity          6497 non-null float64
volatile acidity       6497 non-null float64
citric acid            6497 non-null float64
residual sugar         6497 non-null float64
chlorides              6497 non-null float64
free sulfur dioxide    6497 non-null float64
total sulfur dioxide   6497 non-null float64
density                6497 non-null float64
pH                     6497 non-null float64
sulphates              6497 non-null float64
alcohol                6497 non-null float64
quality                6497 non-null int64
type                   6497 non-null int64
dtypes: float64(11), int64(2)
memory usage: 659.9 KB
```

Figure 31.2: Basic information about the wine quality dataset.

```
X = df.drop('quality', axis=1)
y = df.quality
```

A common part of pre-processing data is feature scaling. Standardization transforms the data so that each feature variable has a zero mean and a variance of 1. The next lines of the code utilise **scikit-learn**'s standard scaler to standardize the feature variables.

```
scaler = StandardScaler().fit(X)
X = scaler.transform(X)
```

Next, we split the dataset into train and test.

```
X_train, X_test, y_train, y_test = \
    train_test_split(X, y, test_size=0.33, random_state=10)
```

Define network

We define the neural network as consisting of a single hidden layer. The layer consists of 64 neurons. Since there are 12 features in the wine dataset, the input dimension

is 12. The activation function for the hidden layer is ReLU. We then define an output
layer with a single layer.

```
model = Sequential()
model.add(Dense(64, input_dim=12, activation='relu'))
model.add(Dense(1))

model.summary()
```

A summary of the model is shown in Figure 31.3. The first layer (hidden layer)
consists of 64 neurons and 832 parameters. The final output layer consists of a single
neuron and 65 parameters. The total number of parameters is 897.

```
Layer (type)              Output Shape            Param #
=================================================================
dense_1 (Dense)           (None, 64)              832

dense_2 (Dense)           (None, 1)               65
=================================================================
Total params: 897
Trainable params: 897
Non-trainable params: 0

```

Figure 31.3: Summary of the deep learning network for wine quality regression.

Compile model and fit data

After setting up the network we compile the model and fit the day. We use the *rmsprop*
optimizer, which is a common optimizer for regression tasks. The loss function is *mse*.
We use 10 epochs for the training.

```
model.compile(optimizer='rmsprop', loss='mse', metrics=['mae'])
model.fit(X_train, y_train, epochs=10, verbose=0)
```

Generate predictions and evaluate model

After developing the model, we predict new data using test. We evaluate the model
using R^2. The model has an R^2 of .35. It's likely that model can be improved with feature
tuning and adjusting hyperparameters, including the architecture of the deep learning
network.

```
y_pred = model.predict(X_test)
r2_score(y_test, y_pred)
```

List of Figures

https://doi.org/10.1515/9781501505737-032

List of Tables

https://doi.org/10.1515/9781501505737-033

About the Authors

Alfred Essa has led advanced analytics, machine learning, and information technology teams in academia and industry. He has served as Simon Fellow at Carnegie Mellon University, VP of Analytics and R&D at McGraw Hill Education, and CIO at MIT's Sloan School of Management. He is a graduate of Haverford College and Yale University.

Shirin Mojarad is a senior machine learning specialist at Google Cloud. Previously, she was a senior data scientist at Apple where she worked on AB experimentation, causal inference, and metrics design. She has experience applying AI and machine learning to five vertical markets in Big Data: healthcare, finance, educational technology, high tech, and cloud technology. She received her master's and Ph.D. from Newcastle University, United Kingdom.

https://doi.org/10.1515/9781501505737-034

Index

https://doi.org/10.1515/9781501505737-035

www.ingramcontent.com/pod-product-compliance
Lightning Source LLC
Chambersburg PA
CBHW080552060326
40689CB00021B/4828